Mathematics 300
Teacher's Guide

CONTENTS

Author: **Carol Bauler, B.A.**
Editor: Alan Christopherson, M.S.
Graphic Design: JoAnn Cumming, A.A.

Alpha Omega Publications ®

804 North 2nd Avenue East, Rock Rapids, Iowa 51246
© MCMXCVIII by Alpha Omega Publications, Inc. All rights reserved.
LIFEPAC is a registered trademark of Alpha Omega Publications, Inc.

MATHEMATICS

Curriculum Overview
Grades K-12

■————————————————————————■

Kindergarten

Lessons

1-40	41-80	81-120	121-160
Directions-right, left, high,low,etc. **Comparisons**-big, little,alike,different **Matching** **Cardinal Numbers**-to 9 **Colors**-red,blue,green, yellow, brown,purple **Shapes**-circle,square, rectangle,triangle **Number Order** **Before and After** **Ordinal Numbers**-to 9th **Problem Solving**	**Directions**-right,left, high,low,etc. **Comparisons**-big, little,alike,different **Matching** **Cardinal Numbers**-to 12 **Colors**-orange **Shapes**-circle,square, rectangle,triangle **Number Order** **Before and After** **Ordinal Numbers**-to 9th **Problem Solving** **Number Words**-to nine **Addition**-to 9	**Directions**-right,left, high,low,etc. **Comparisons**-big, little,alike,different **Matching** **Cardinal Numbers**-to 19 **Colors**-black,white **Shapes**-circle square, rectangle,triangle **Number Order** **Before and After** **Ordinal Numbers**-to 9th **Problem Solving** **Number Words**-to nine **Addition**-to 10 and multiples of 10 **Subtraction**-to 9 **Place Value** **Time/Calendar**	**Directions**-right,left, high,low,etc. **Comparisons**-big, little,alike,different **Matching** **Cardinal Numbers**-to 100 **Colors**-pink **Shapes**-circle,square, rectangle,triangle **Number Order** **Before and After** **Ordinal Numbers**-to 9th **Problem Solving** **Number Words**-to nine **Addition**-to 10 and multiples of 10 **Subtraction**-to 10 **Place Value** **Time/Calendar** **Money** **Skip Counting**-2's, 5's, 10's **Greater/ Less than**

Mathematics LIFEPAC Overview

	Grade 1	Grade 2	Grade 3
LIFEPAC 1	**NUMBERS TO 99** • Number order, skip-count • Add, subtract to 9 • Story problems • Measurements, shapes	**NUMBERS TO 100** • Numbers and words to 100 • Operation symbols +, −, =, >, < • Add, subtract, story problems • Place value, fact families	**NUMBERS TO 999** • Digits, place value to 999 • Add, subtract, time • Linear measurements, dozen • Operation symbols +, −, =, ≠, >, <
LIFEPAC 2	**NUMBERS TO 99** • Add, subtract to 10 • Number words • Place value, shapes • Patterns, sequencing, estimation	**NUMBERS TO 200** • Numbers and words to 200 • Add, subtract, even and odd • Skip-count 2's, 5's, 10's, shapes • Ordinal numbers, fractions, money	**NUMBERS TO 999** • Fact families, patterns, fractions • Add, subtract - carry, borrow • Skip count 2's, 5's, 10's • Money, shapes, lines, even, odd
LIFEPAC 3	**NUMBERS TO 100** • Number sentences, • Fractions, oral directions • Story problems • Time, symbols =, ≠	**NUMBERS TO 200** • Add w/ carry to 10's place • Subtract, standard measurements • Flat shapes, money, AM/PM • Rounding to 10's place	**NUMBERS TO 999** • Add 3 numbers w/ carry • Coins, weight, volume, AM/PM • Fractions, oral instructions • Skip count 3's, subtract w/ borrow
LIFEPAC 4	**NUMBERS TO 100** • Add to 18, place value • Skip-count, even and odd • Money • Shapes, measurement	**NUMBERS TO 999** • Numbers and words to 999 • Add, subtract, place value • Calendar, making change • Measurements, solid shapes	**NUMBERS TO 9,999** • Place value to 9,999 • Rounding to 10's, estimation • Add and subtract fractions • Roman numerals, 1/4 inch
LIFEPAC 5	**NUMBERS TO 100** • Add 3 numbers - 1 digit • Ordinal numbers, fractions • Time, number line • Estimation, charts	**NUMBERS TO 999** • Data and bar graphs, shapes • Add, subtract to 100's • Skip-count 3's, place value to 100's • Add fractions, temperature	**NUMBERS TO 9,999** • Number sentences, temperature • Rounding to 100's, estimation • Perimeter, square inch • Bar graph, symmetry, even/odd rules
LIFEPAC 6	**NUMBERS TO 100** • Number words to 99 • Add 2 numbers - 2 digit • Symbols >, < • Fractions, shapes	**NUMBERS TO 999** • Measurements, perimeter • Time, money • Subtract w/ borrow from 10's place • Add, subtract fractions	**NUMBERS TO 9,999** • Add, subtract to 9,999 • Multiples, times facts for 2 • Area, equivalent fractions, money • Line graph, segments, angles
LIFEPAC 7	**NUMBERS TO 200** • Number order, place value • Subtract to 12 • Operation signs • Estimation, graphs, time	**NUMBERS TO 999** • Add w/ carry to 100's place • Fractions as words • Number order in books • Rounding and estimation	**NUMBERS TO 9,999** • Times facts for 5, missing numbers • Mixed numbers - add, subtract • Subtract with 0's in minuend • Circle graph, probability
LIFEPAC 8	**NUMBERS TO 200** • Addition, subtract to 18 • Group counting • Fractions, shapes • Time, measurements	**NUMBERS TO 999** • Add, subtract, measurements • Group count, 'think' answers • Convert coins, length, width • Directions-N, S, E, W	**NUMBERS TO 9,999** • Times facts for 3, 10 - multiples of 4 • Convert units of measurement • Decimals, directions, length, width • Picture graph, missing addend
LIFEPAC 9	**NUMBERS TO 200** • Add 3 numbers - 2 digit • Fact families • Sensible answers • Subtract 2 numbers - 2 digit	**NUMBERS TO 999** • Area and square measurement • Add 3 numbers - 2 digit w/ carry • Add coins and convert to cents • Fractions, quarter-inch	**NUMBERS TO 9,999** • Add, subtract whole numbers, fractions, mixed numbers • Standard measurements, metrics • Operation symbols, times facts for 4
LIFEPAC 10	**NUMBERS TO 200** • Add, subtract, place value • Directions - N, S, E, W • Fractions • Patterns	**NUMBERS TO 999** • Rules for even and odd • Round numbers to 100's place • Time - digital, sensible answers • Add 3 numbers - 3 digit	**NUMBERS TO 9,999** • Add, subtract, times facts 2,3,4,5,10 • Rounding to 1,000's, estimation • Probability, equations, parentheses • Perimeter, area

Grade 4	Grade 5	Grade 6	
WHOLE NUMBERS & FRACTIONS • Naming whole numbers • Naming Fractions • Sequencing patterns • Numbers to 1,000	**WHOLE NUMBERS & FRACTIONS** • Operations & symbols • Fraction language • Grouping, patterns, sequencing • Rounding & estimation	**FRACTIONS & DECIMALS** • Number to billions' place • Add & subtract fractions • Add & subtract decimals • Read and write Fractions	LIFEPAC 1
WHOLE NUMBERS & FRACTIONS • Operation symbols • Multiplication - 1 digit multiplier • Fractions - addition & subtraction • Numbers to 10,000	**WHOLE NUMBERS & FRACTIONS** • Multiplication & division • Fractions - +, –, simplify • Plane & solid shapes • Symbol language	**FINDING COMMON DENOMINATORS** • Prime factors • Fractions with unlike denominators • Exponential notation • Add & subtract mixed numbers	LIFEPAC 2
WHOLE NUMBERS & FRACTIONS • Multiplication with carrying • Rounding & estimation • Sequencing fractions • Numbers to 100,000	**WHOLE NUMBERS & FRACTIONS** • Short division • Lowest common multiple • Perimeter & area • Properties of addition	**MULTIPLYING MIXED NUMBERS** • Multiply mixed numbers • Divide decimals • Bar and line graphs • Converting fractions & decimals	LIFEPAC 3
LINES & SHAPES • Plane & solid shapes • Lines & line segments • Addition & subtraction • Multiplication with carrying	**WHOLE NUMBERS** • Lines - shapes - circles • Symmetric - congruent - similar • Decimal place value • Properties of multiplication	**DIVIDING MIXED NUMBERS** • Divide mixed numbers • Area and perimeter • Standard measurements	LIFEPAC 4
WHOLE NUMBERS • Division - 1 digit divisor • Families of facts • Standard measurements • Number grouping	**WHOLE NUMBERS & FRACTIONS** • Multiply & divide by 10, 100, 1,000 • Standard measurements • Rate problems • Whole number & fraction operations	**METRIC MEASURE** • Metric measures • Plane & solid shapes • Multi-operation problems • Roman Numerals	LIFEPAC 5
WHOLE NUMBERS & FRACTIONS • Division - 1 digit with remainder • Factors & multiples • Fractions - improper & mixed • Equivalent fractions	**FRACTIONS & DECIMALS** • Multiplication of fractions • Reading decimal numbers • Adding & subtracting decimals • Multiplication - decimals	**LCM & GCF** • LCM, GCF • Fraction and decimal equivalents • Percent • Variables, functions & formulas	LIFEPAC 6
WHOLE NUMBERS & FRACTIONS • Multiplication - 2 digit multiplier • Simplifying fractions • Averages • Decimals in money problems	**WHOLE NUMBERS & FRACTIONS** • Division - 2-digit divisor • Metric units • Multiplication - mixed numbers • Multiplication - decimals	**INTEGERS, RATIO & PROPORTION** • Positive and negative integers • Ratio & proportion • Fractions, decimals & percents • Statistics	LIFEPAC 7
WHOLE NUMBERS & FRACTIONS • Division 1 digit divisor • Fractions - unlike denominators • Metric units • Whole numbers - +, –, x, ÷	**WHOLE NUMBERS** • Calculators & whole numbers • Calculators & decimals • Estimation • Prime factors	**PROBABILITY & GRAPHING** • Probability • Graphs • Metric and standard units • Square root	LIFEPAC 8
DECIMALS & FRACTIONS • Reading and writing decimals • Mixed numbers - +, – • Cross multiplication • Estimation	**FRACTIONS & DECIMALS** • Division - fractions • Division - decimals • Ratios & ordered pairs • Converting fractions to decimals	**CALCULATORS & ESTIMATION** • Calculators • Estimation • Geometric symbols & shapes • Missing number problems	LIFEPAC 9
PROBLEM SOLVING • Estimation & data gathering • Charts & Graphs • Review numbers to 100,000 • Whole numbers - +, –, x, ÷	**PROBLEM SOLVING** • Probability & data gathering • Charts & graphs • Review numbers to 100 million • Fractions & decimals - +, –, x, ÷	**INTEGERS & OPERATIONS** • Mental arithmetic • Fraction operations • Variables & properties • Number lines	LIFEPAC 10

7

Mathematics LIFEPAC Overview

	Grade 7	Grade 8	Grade 9
LIFEPAC 1	**WHOLE NUMBERS** • Number concepts • Addition • Subtraction • Applications	**WHOLE NUMBERS** • The set of whole numbers • Graphs • Operations with whole numbers • Applications with whole numbers	**VARIABLES AND NUMBERS** • Variables • Distributive Property • Definition of signed numbers • Signed number operations
LIFEPAC 2	**MULTIPLICATION AND DIVISION** • Basic facts • Procedures • Practice • Applications	**NUMBERS AND FACTORS** • Numbers and bases • Sets • Factors and multiples • Least common multiples	**SOLVING EQUATIONS** • Sentences and formulas • Properties • Solving equations • Solving inequalities
LIFEPAC 3	**GEOMETRY** • Segments, lines, and angles • Triangles • Quadrilaterals • Circles and hexagons	**RATIONAL NUMBERS** • Proper and improper fractions • Mixed numbers • Decimal fractions • Per cent	**PROBLEM ANALYSIS AND SOLUTION** • Words and symbols • Simple verbal problems • Medium verbal problems • Challenging verbal problems
LIFEPAC 4	**RATIONAL NUMBERS** • Common fractions • Improper fractions • Mixed numbers • Decimal fractions	**FRACTIONS AND ROUNDING** • Common fraction addition • Common fraction subtraction • Decimal fractions • Rounding numbers	**POLYNOMIALS** • Addition of polynomials • Subtraction of polynomials • Multiplication of polynomials • Division of polynomials
LIFEPAC 5	**SETS AND NUMBERS** • Set concepts and operations • Early number systems • Decimal number system • Factors and multiples	**FRACTIONS AND PER CENT** • Multiplication of fractions • Division of fractions • Fractions as per cents • Per cent exercises	**ALGEBRAIC FACTORS** • Greatest common factor • Binomial factors • Complete factorization • Word problems
LIFEPAC 6	**FRACTIONS** • Like denominators • Unlike denominators • Decimal fractions • Equivalents	**STATISTICS, GRAPHS, & PROBABILITY** • Statistical measures • Types of graphs • Simple probability • And–Or statements	**ALGEBRAIC FRACTIONS** • Operations with fractions • Solving equations • Solving inequalities • Solving word problems
LIFEPAC 7	**FRACTIONS** • Common fractions • Decimal fractions • Per cent • Word problems	**INTEGERS** • Basic concepts • Addition and subtraction • Multiplication and division • Expressions and sentences	**RADICAL EXPRESSIONS** • Rational and irrational numbers • Operations with radicals • Irrational roots • Radical equations
LIFEPAC 8	**FORMULAS AND RATIOS** • Writing formulas • A function machine • Equations • Ratios and proportions	**FORMULAS AND GEOMETRY** • Square root • Perimeter, circumference, and area • Rectangular solid • Cylinder, cone, and sphere	**GRAPHING** • Equations of two variables • Graphing lines • Graphing inequalities • Equations of lines
LIFEPAC 9	**DATA, STATISTICS AND GRAPHS** • Gathering and organizing data • Central tendency and dispersion • Graphs of statistics • Graphs of points	**ALGEBRAIC EQUATIONS** • Variables in formulas • Addition and subtraction • Multiplication and division • Problem solving	**SYSTEMS** • Graphical solution • Algebraic solutions • Determinants • Word problems
LIFEPAC 10	**MATHEMATICS IN SPORTS** • Whole numbers • Geometry, sets, and systems • Fractions • Formulas, ratios, and statistics	**NUMBERS, FRACTIONS, ALGEBRA** • Whole numbers and fractions • Fractions and per cent • Statistics, graphs and probability • Integers and algebra	**QUADRATIC EQUATIONS AND REVIEW** • Solving quadratic equations • Equations and inequalities • Polynomials and factors • Radicals and graphing

Grade 10	Grade 11	Grade 12	
A MATHEMATICAL SYSTEM • Points, lines, and planes • Definition of definitions • Geometric terms • Postulates and theorems	**SETS, STRUCTURE, AND FUNCTION** • Properties and operations of sets • Axioms and applications • Relations and functions • Algebraic expressions	**RELATIONS AND FUNCTIONS** • Relations and functions • Rules of correspondence • Notation of functions • Types of functions	LIFEPAC 1
PROOFS • Logic • Reasoning • Two-column proof • Paragraph proof	**NUMBERS, SENTENCES, & PROBLEMS** • Order and absolute value • Sums and products • Algebraic sentences • Number and motion problems	**SPECIAL FUNCTIONS** • Linear functions • Second-degree functions • Polynomial functions • Other functions	LIFEPAC 2
ANGLES AND PARALLELS • Definitions and measurement • Relationships and theorems • Properties of parallels • Parallels and polygons	**LINEAR EQUATIONS & INEQUALITIES** • Graphs • Equations • Systems of equations • Inequalities	**TRIGONOMETRIC FUNCTIONS** • Definition • Evaluation of functions • Trigonometric tables • Special angles	LIFEPAC 3
CONGRUENCY • Congruent triangles • Corresponding parts • Inequalities • Quadrilaterals	**POLYNOMIALS** • Multiplying polynomials • Factoring • Operations with polynomials • Variations	**CIRCULAR FUNCTIONS & GRAPHS** • Circular functions & special angles • Graphs of sin and cos • Amplitude and period • Phase shifts	LIFEPAC 4
SIMILAR POLYGONS • Ratios and proportions • Definition of similarity • Similar polygons and triangles • Right triangle geometry	**RADICAL EXPRESSIONS** • Multiplying and dividing fractions • Adding and subtracting fractions • Equations with fractions • Applications of fractions	**IDENTITIES AND FUNCTIONS** • Reciprocal relations • Pythagorean relations • Trigonometric identities • Sum and difference formulas	LIFEPAC 5
CIRCLES • Circles and spheres • Tangents, arcs, and chords • Special angles in circles • Special segments in circles	**REAL NUMBERS** • Rational and irrational numbers • Laws of Radicals • Quadratic equations • Quadratic formula	**TRIGONOMETRIC FUNCTIONS** • Trigonometric functions • Law of cosines • Law of sines • Applied problems	LIFEPAC 6
CONSTRUCTION AND LOCUS • Basic constructions • Triangles and circles • Polygons • Locus meaning and use	**QUADRATIC RELATIONS & SYSTEMS** • Distance formulas • Conic sections • Systems of equations • Application of conic sections	**TRIGONOMETRIC FUNCTIONS** • Inverse functions • Graphing polar coordinates • Converting polar coordinates • Graphing polar equations	LIFEPAC 7
AREA AND VOLUME • Area of polygons • Area of circles • Surface area of solids • Volume of solids	**EXPONENTIAL FUNCTIONS** • Exponents • Exponential equations • Logarithmic functions • Matrices	**QUADRATIC EQUATIONS** • Conic sections • Circle and ellipse • Parabola and hyperbola • Transformations	LIFEPAC 8
COORDINATE GEOMETRY • Ordered pairs • Distance • Lines • Coordinate proofs	**COUNTING PRINCIPLES** • Progressions • Permutations • Combinations • Probability	**PROBABILITY** • Random experiments & probability • Permutations • Combinations • Applied problems	LIFEPAC 9
REVIEW • Proof and angles • Polygons and circles • Construction and measurement • Coordinate geometry	**REVIEW** • Integers and open sentences • Graphs and polynomials • Fractions and quadratics • Exponential functions	**CALCULUS** • Mathematical induction • Functions and limits • Slopes of functions • Review of 1200 mathematics	LIFEPAC 10

MANAGEMENT

STRUCTURE OF THE LIFEPAC CURRICULUM

The LIFEPAC curriculum is conveniently structured to provide one teacher handbook containing teacher support material with answer keys and ten student worktexts for each subject at grade levels two through twelve. The worktext format of the LIFEPACs allows the student to read the textual information and complete workbook activities all in the same booklet. The easy to follow LIFEPAC numbering system lists the grade as the first number(s) and the last two digits as the number of the series. For example, the Language Arts LIFEPAC at the 6th grade level, 5th book in the series would be LA 605.

Each LIFEPAC is divided into 3 to 5 sections and begins with an introduction or overview of the booklet as well as a series of specific learning objectives to give a purpose to the study of the LIFEPAC. The introduction and objectives are followed by a vocabulary section which may be found at the beginning of each section at the lower levels, at the beginning of the LIFEPAC in the middle grades, or in the glossary at the high school level. Vocabulary words are used to develop word recognition and should not be confused with the spelling words introduced later in the LIFEPAC. The student should learn all vocabulary words before working the LIFEPAC sections to improve comprehension, retention, and reading skills.

Each activity or written assignment has a number for easy identification, such as 1.1. The first number corresponds to the LIFEPAC section and the number to the right of the decimal is the number of the activity.

Teacher checkpoints, which are essential to maintain quality learning, are found at various locations throughout the LIFEPAC. The teacher should check 1) neatness of work and penmanship, 2) quality of understanding (tested with a short oral quiz), 3) thoroughness of answers (complete sentences and paragraphs, correct spelling, etc.), 4) completion of activities (no blank spaces), and 5) accuracy of answers as compared to the answer key (all answers correct).

The self test questions are also number coded for easy reference. For example, 2.015 means that this is the 15th question in the self test of Section II. The first number corresponds to the LIFEPAC section, the zero indicates that it is a self test question, and the number to the right of the zero the question number.

The LIFEPAC test is packaged at the centerfold of each LIFEPAC. It should be removed and put aside before giving the booklet to the student for study.

Answer and test keys have the same numbering system as the LIFEPACs and appear at the back of this handbook. The student may be given access to the answer keys (not the test keys) under teacher supervision so that he can score his own work.

A thorough study of the Curriculum Overview by the teacher before instruction begins is essential to the success of the student. The teacher should become familiar with expected skill mastery and understand how these grade level skills fit into the overall skill development of the curriculum. The teacher should also preview the objectives that appear at the beginning of each LIFEPAC for additional preparation and planning.

TEST SCORING and GRADING

Answer keys and test keys give examples of correct answers. They convey the idea, but the student may use many ways to express a correct answer. The teacher should check for the essence of the answer, not for the exact wording. Many questions are high level and require thinking and creativity on the part of the student. Each answer should be scored based on whether or not the main idea written by the student matches the model example. "Any Order" or "Either Order" in a key indicates that no particular order is necessary to be correct.

Most self tests and LIFEPAC tests at the lower elementary levels are scored at 1 point per question; however, the upper levels may have a point system awarding 2 to 5 points for various questions. Further, the total test points will vary; they may not always equal 100 points. They may be 78, 85, 100, 105, etc.

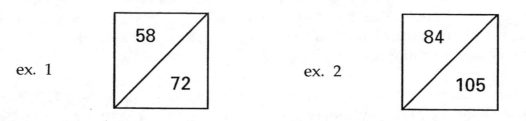

A score box similar to ex.1 above is located at the end of each self test and on the front of the LIFEPAC test. The bottom score, 72, represents the total number of points possible on the test. The upper score, 58, represents the number of points your student will need to receive an 80% or passing grade. If you wish to establish the exact percentage that your student has achieved, find the total points of his correct answers and divide it by the bottom number (in this case 72.) For example, if your student has a point total of 65, divide 65 by 72 for a grade of 90%. Referring to ex. 2, on a test with a total of 105 possible points, the student would have to receive a minimum of 84 correct points for an 80% or passing grade. If your student has received 93 points, simply divide the 93 by 105 for a percentage grade of 89%. Students who receive a score below 80% should review the LIFEPAC and retest using the appropriate Alternate Test found in the Teacher's Guide.

The following is a guideline to assign letter grades for completed LIFEPACs based on a maximum total score of 100 points.

LIFEPAC Test = 60% of the Total Score (or percent grade)
Self Test = 25% of the Total Score (average percent of self tests)
Reports = 10% or 10* points per LIFEPAC
Oral Work = 5% or 5* points per LIFEPAC
*Determined by the teacher's subjective evaluation of the student's daily work.

Example:

LIFEPAC Test Score	=	92%	92	x	.60	=	55 points
Self Test Average	=	90%	90	x	.25	=	23 points
Reports						=	8 points
Oral Work						=	4 points

TOTAL POINTS   =   90 points

Grade Scale based on point system:

100	–	94	=	A
93	–	86	=	B
85	–	77	=	C
76	–	70	=	D
Below		70	=	F

TEACHER HINTS and STUDYING TECHNIQUES

LIFEPAC Activities are written to check the level of understanding of the preceding text. The student may look back to the text as necessary to complete these activities; however, a student should never attempt to do the activities without reading (studying) the text first. Self tests and LIFEPAC tests are never open book tests.

Language arts activities (skill integration) often appear within other subject curriculum. The purpose is to give the student an opportunity to test his skill mastery outside of the context in which it was presented.

Writing complete answers (paragraphs) to some questions is an integral part of the LIFEPAC Curriculum in all subjects. This builds communication and organization skills, increases understanding and retention of ideas, and helps enforce good penmanship. Complete sentences should be encouraged for this type of activity. Obviously, single words or phrases do not meet the intent of the activity, since multiple lines are given for the response.

Review is essential to student success. Time invested in review where review is suggested will be time saved in correcting errors later. Self tests, unlike the section activities, are closed book. This procedure helps to identify weaknesses before they become too great to overcome. Certain objectives from self tests are cumulative and test previous sections; therefore, good preparation for a self test must include all material studied up to that testing point.

The following procedure checklist has been found to be successful in developing good study habits in the LIFEPAC curriculum.

1. Read the introduction and Table of Contents.
2. Read the objectives.
3. Recite and study the entire vocabulary (glossary) list.
4. Study each section as follows:
    a. Read the introduction and study the section objectives.
    b. Read all the text for the entire section, but answer none of the activities.
    c. Return to the beginning of the section and memorize each vocabulary word and definition.
    d. Reread the section, complete the activities, check the answers with the answer key, correct all errors, and have the teacher check.
    e. Read the self test but do not answer the questions.
    f. Go to the beginning of the first section and reread the text and answers to the activities up to the self test you have not yet done.
    g. Answer the questions to the self test without looking back.
    h. Have the self test checked by the teacher.
    i. Correct the self test and have the teacher check the corrections.
    j. Repeat steps a–i for each section.

5. Use the SQ3R* method to prepare for the LIFEPAC test.
6. Take the LIFEPAC test as a closed book test.
7. LIFEPAC tests are administered and scored under direct teacher supervision. Students who receive scores below 80% should review the LIFEPAC using the SQ3R* study method and take the Alternate Test located in the Teacher Handbook. The final test grade may be the grade on the Alternate Test or an average of the grades from the original LIFEPAC test and the Alternate Test.

  *SQ3R: Scan the whole LIFEPAC.
     Question yourself on the objectives.
     Read the whole LIFEPAC again.
     Recite through an oral examination.
     Review weak areas.

GOAL SETTING and SCHEDULES

Each school must develop its own schedule, because no single set of procedures will fit every situation. The following is an example of a daily schedule that includes the five LIFEPAC subjects as well as time slotted for special activities.

Possible Daily Schedule

8:15	–	8:25	Pledges, prayer, songs, devotions, etc.
8:25	–	9:10	Bible
9:10	–	9:55	Language Arts
9:55	–	10:15	Recess (juice break)
10:15	–	11:00	Mathematics
11:00	–	11:45	Social Studies
11:45	–	12:30	Lunch, recess, quiet time
12:30	–	1:15	Science
1:15	–		Drill, remedial work, enrichment*

*Enrichment: Computer time, physical education, field trips, fun reading, games and puzzles, family business, hobbies, resource persons, guests, crafts, creative work, electives, music appreciation, projects.

Basically, two factors need to be considered when assigning work to a student in the LIFEPAC curriculum.

The first is time. An average of 45 minutes should be devoted to each subject, each day. Remember, this is only an average. Because of extenuating circumstances a student may spend only 15 minutes on a subject one day and the next day spend 90 minutes on the same subject.

The second factor is the number of pages to be worked in each subject. A single LIFEPAC is designed to take 3 to 4 weeks to complete. Allowing about 3-4 days for LIFEPAC introduction, review, and tests, the student has approximately 15 days to complete the LIFEPAC pages. Simply take the number of pages in the LIFEPAC, divide it by 15 and you will have the number of pages that must be completed on a daily basis to keep the student on schedule. For example, a LIFEPAC containing 45 pages will require 3 completed pages per day. Again, this is only an average. While working a 45 page LIFEPAC, the student may complete only 1 page the first day if the text has a lot of activities or reports, but go on to complete 5 pages the next day.

Long range planning requires some organization. Because the traditional school year originates in the early fall of one year and continues to late spring of the following year, a calendar should be devised that covers this period of time. Approximate beginning and completion dates can be noted on the calendar as well as special occasions such as holidays, vacations, and birthdays. Since each LIFEPAC takes 3-4 weeks or eighteen days to complete, it should take about 180 school days to finish a set of ten LIFEPACs. Starting at the beginning school date, mark off eighteen school days on the calendar and that will become the targeted completion date for the first LIFEPAC. Continue marking the calendar until you have established dates for the remaining nine LIFEPACs making adjustments for previously noted holidays and vacations. If all five subjects are being used, the ten established target dates should be the same for the LIFEPACs in each subject.

FORMS

The sample weekly lesson plan and student grading sheet forms are included in this section as teacher support materials and may be duplicated at the convenience of the teacher.

The student grading sheet is provided for those who desire to follow the suggested guidelines for assignment of letter grades found on page 15 of this section. The student's self test scores should be posted as percentage grades. When the LIFEPAC is completed the teacher should average the self test grades, multiply the average by .25 and post the points in the box marked self test points. The LIFEPAC percentage grade should be multiplied by .60 and posted. Next, the teacher should award and post points for written reports and oral work. A report may be any type of written work assigned to the student whether it is a LIFEPAC or additional learning activity. Oral work includes the student's ability to respond orally to questions which may or may not be related to LIFEPAC activities or any type of oral report assigned by the teacher. The points may then be totaled and a final grade entered along with the date that the LIFEPAC was completed.

The Student Record Book which was specifically designed for use with the Alpha Omega curriculum provides space to record weekly progress for one student over a nine week period as well as a place to post self test and LIFEPAC scores. The Student Record Books are available through the current Alpha Omega catalog; however, unlike the enclosed forms these books are not for duplication and should be purchased in sets of four to cover a full academic year.

WEEKLY LESSON PLANNER

Week of:

	Subject	Subject	Subject	Subject
Monday				
Tuesday	Subject /	Subject	Subject	Subject
Wednesday	Subject	Subject	Subject	Subject
Thursday	Subject	Subject	Subject	Subject
Friday	Subject	Subject	Subject	Subject

WEEKLY LESSON PLANNER

Week of:

	Subject	Subject	Subject	Subject
Monday				

	Subject	Subject	Subject	Subject
Tuesday				

	Subject	Subject	Subject	Subject
Wednesday				

	Subject	Subject	Subject	Subject
Thursday				

	Subject	Subject	Subject	Subject
Friday				

Student Name _____   Year _____

Bible

LP #	Self Test Scores by Sections 1	2	3	4	5	Self Test Points	LIFEPAC Test	Oral Points	Report Points	Final Grade	Date
01											
02											
03											
04											
05											
06											
07											
08											
09											
10											

Language Arts

LP #	Self Test Scores by Sections 1	2	3	4	5	Self Test Points	LIFEPAC Test	Oral Points	Report Points	Final Grade	Date
01											
02											
03											
04											
05											
06											
07											
08											
09											
10											

Mathematics

LP #	Self Test Scores by Sections 1	2	3	4	5	Self Test Points	LIFEPAC Test	Oral Points	Report Points	Final Grade	Date
01											
02											
03											
04											
05											
06											
07											
08											
09											
10											

Student Name _____   Year _____

Science

LP #	Self Test Scores by Sections 1	2	3	4	5	Self Test Points	LIFEPAC Test	Oral Points	Report Points	Final Grade	Date
01											
02											
03											
04											
05											
06											
07											
08											
09											
10											

Social Studies

LP #	Self Test Scores by Sections 1	2	3	4	5	Self Test Points	LIFEPAC Test	Oral Points	Report Points	Final Grade	Date
01											
02											
03											
04											
05											
06											
07											
08											
09											
10											

Spelling/Electives

LP #	Self Test Scores by Sections 1	2	3	4	5	Self Test Points	LIFEPAC Test	Oral Points	Report Points	Final Grade	Date
01											
02											
03											
04											
05											
06											
07											
08											
09											
10											

NOTES

INSTRUCTIONS FOR THIRD GRADE MATHEMATICS

The LIFEPAC curriculum for grades two through twelve is structured so that the daily instructional material is written directly into the LIFEPACs. However, because of the variety of reading abilities at this grade level, the third grade mathematics Teacher's Guide contains additional instructional material to help the teacher prepare and present each lesson effectively. As the year progresses, students should be encouraged to read and follow the instructional material as presented in the LIFEPACs to develop independent study habits. The teacher should introduce the LIFEPAC to the student, set a required completion schedule, complete teacher checks, be available for questions regarding both content and procedures, administer and grade tests, and develop additional learning activities as desired. Teachers working with several students may schedule their time so that students are assigned to a quiet work activity when it is necessary to spend instructional time with one particular student.

This section of the Teacher's Guide includes the following teacher aids: 1) Introduction of Skills 2) Mathematics Terms 3) Teacher Instruction Pages 4) Additional Activities.

The Introduction of Skills is a more detailed overview of skills than that presented in the *Scope and Sequence*. The Mathematics Terms includes a glossary of mathematics terms and a table of measurements. The Teacher Instruction Pages contain guidelines for teaching each lesson. Additional learning activities provide opportunities for problem solving, encourage the student's interest in learning, and may be used as a reward for good study habits.

Mathematics is a subject that requires skill mastery. But skill mastery needs to be applied toward active student involvement. The Teacher Instruction Pages list the required or suggested materials used in the LIFEPAC lessons. These materials include items generally available in the school or home. Pencils, paper, crayons, scissors, paste and/or glue stick are materials used on a regular basis. Construction paper, beads, buttons, and beans can be used for counting, sets, grouping, fractions, and patterning. Measurements require measuring cups, rulers, and empty containers. Boxes and similar items help in the study of solid shapes.

Any workbook assignment that can be supported by a real world experience will enhance the student's ability for problem solving. There is an infinite challenge for the teacher to provide a meaningful environment for the study of mathematics. It is a subject that requires constant assessment of student progress. Do not leave the study of mathematics in the classroom.

INTRODUCTION OF SKILLS

Introduction of Skills is a quick reference guide for the teacher who may be looking for a rule or explanation that applies to a particular skill or to find where or when certain skills are introduced in the LIFEPACs. The first number after the skill identifies the LIFEPAC, and the second number identifies the section. 305/3 refers to Mathematics LIFEPAC 305, Section 3.

Addition

facts to 18	301/1	
3 numbers 1-digit	302/1	*n/c no carrying
2 numbers 2, 3-digits n/c	301/2,3	
2 numbers 4-digit n/c	306/1	*w/c with carrying
3 numbers 2-digit n/c	303/1	
3 numbers 3-digit n/c	304/1	
2 numbers 2-digits w/c	301/4	
2 numbers 3-digits w/c	302/2	
2 numbers 4-digits w/c	306/1	
3 numbers 2-digits w/c	303/1	
3 numbers 3-digits w/c	305/2	
checking answers	302/4	
sum, addend	301/2	

Decimals

used in money	302/4
to tenths	308/2

Digits

as number symbols	301/5

Directions

north, south, east, west	308/3

Even and odd

numbers	302/3
rules to add and subtract	305/4

Expanding numbers

see place value

Families of facts

addition and subtraction	302/1

Fractions

addition and subtraction	304/4
equal to one whole	309/1
equivalent fractions	306/3
mixed numbers	
in words	307/1
addition and subtraction	307/2
numerator, denominator, fraction bar	302/3
part of an object or set	302/3
writing in words	302/3

Geometry

flat (plane) shapes 302/4

lines, closed and curved, end points 302/4

line segment, angle 306/4

solid shapes 302/4

symmetry 305/3

Graphs (Charts)

gathering and posting data 305/2

bar 305/2

line 306/4

circle 307/3

picture 308/3

Measurements - standard

area 306/2

dozen 301/3

length, width 308/4

linear

inches, feet, yards 301/3

miles 306/2

perimeter 305/3

ruler

to quarter-inch 304/2

square measurement 305/3

temperature (Fahrenheit) 305/2

time

to hour, half-hour, minute 301/4

AM, PM 303/4

digital clock 301/4

calendar - days, weeks, ... 301/4
months, years

volume - cups, pints, quarts, gallons 303/2

weight - ounces, pounds, tons 303/2

Measurements - metric

Celsius (temperature) 309/2

liter, gram 309/4

Missing number problems

addition 307/4

subtraction 310/19

Money

add and subtract 306/18

coins, dollars 302/4

dollar and cent signs, decimal point 302/4

making change 308/2

Multiplication
    facts
        for 2   306/4
        for 5   307/1
        for 3 and 10   308/4
        for 4   309/3
    multiples
        of 2, 5, 10   302/2
        of 3   303/3
        of 4   308/4
    operation signs (x, times)   306/4

Number line
    add or subtract to 20   301/1

Number order
    to 999   301/1
    to 9,999   304/3
    to 10,000   309/4

Number sentences
    operation symbols as words   305/1

Number words
    to nine hundred ninety-nine   301/1
    to nine thousand, nine hundred ninety-nine   301/1
    ten thousand   309/4

Operation symbols
    +, -, =, ≠, >, <   301/4
    x   306/4

Ordinal numbers
    to tenth   301/4
    to ninety-ninth   305/1

Place value
    ones, tens, hundreds   301/2
    thousands   304/3

Problem solving
    adding or subtracting up to
        4-digits `mentally'   301/2
    equations   310/5
    estimation
        add rounded numbers   304/2
        subtract rounded numbers   307/4
    parentheses   310/5
    patterns   302/1
    probability   307/2
    sensible answers   306/2

Roman numerals   304/4

Rounding

to nearest 10	304/2
to nearest 100	305/3
to nearest 1,000	309/23

Story problems   all LIFEPACs Section 5

Subtraction

facts to 18	301/1	
2 numbers 2-digits n/b	301/2	*n/b no borrowing
2 numbers 3-digits n/b	301/3	
2 numbers 4-digits n/b	306/2	
2 numbers 2-digits w/b	302/3	*w/b with borrowing
2 numbers 3-digits w/b 10's or 100's	303/3	
2 numbers 3-digits w/b 10's and 100's	304/2	
2 numbers 4-digit w/b	307/1	
from 0	307/2	
checking answers	302/3	
minuend, subtrahend, difference	301/2	

Zero as a place holder   301/2

MATHEMATICS TERMS

acute angle An angle that is less than a right angle or less than 90 degrees.

addend A number to be added in an addition problem.

angle The distance between two rays or line segments with a common end point.

associative property No matter how numbers are grouped in addition and multiplication, the answer is always the same.

area The measurement of a flat surface. $A = l \times w$ (rectangle) $A = \pi r^2$ (circle)
$A = \frac{1}{2} b \times h$ (triangle)

average The total of a group divided by the number in the group.

bar graph A graph that uses bars to show data.

base The bottom part of a geometric figure on which the figure rests.
The number used as a factor in exponential notation.

cancelling Simplifying a problem in multiplication or division of fractions within the problem.

cardinal numbers Numbers used for counting. 1, 2, 3, 4.....

Celsius Metric unit of measurement for temperature. Freezing 0° C., Boiling 100 °C.

chart An arrangement of data in a logical order.

circle A continuous closed line always the same distance from a center point.

circle graph A circular graph that always represents the whole of the data.

circumference The distance around (perimeter) a circle. $C = 2\pi r$ or $C = \pi d$

common denominator Fractions must have the same or common denominator to be added or subtracted.

compass An instrument having two hinged legs used for drawing circles, curved lines, and measuring distances.

composite number A number that can be divided by 1, by itself, and other numbers.

commutative property No matter what order numbers are added or multiplied, the answer is always the same.

congruent Figures that have the same size and shape.

cross multiplication Multiplying the numerators and denominators of two fractions.

cube A solid shape with six square faces.

cylinder A round shape with flat ends.

data A list of facts from which a conclusion may be drawn.

decimal number A fraction with an understood denominator of 10, 100, 1,000...

decimal point A dot separating the whole number from the fractional part of a decimal number.

degree The unit of measurement for angles.

denominator The bottom number of a fraction. This number represents the whole.

diameter The distance across a circle straight through the middle.

difference The answer to a subtraction problem.

digit Symbols 0, 1, 2, 3, 4, 5 ,6, 7, 8, 9 which when used alone or in combinations represent a value.

division bar The line that separates the numerator from the denominator of a fraction.

divisor The number doing the dividing in a division problem.

dividend The number being divided in a division problem.

end points Dots that show the beginning and end of a line segment.

equal to Has the same value as.   equal = (not equal ≠)

equation   A number sentence that contains an equal sign.

equilateral triangle   A triangle whose sides are all equal in length.

equivalent fractions   Two or more fractions of equal value. To make an equivalent fraction, multiply or divide the numerator and denominator by the same number.

estimate   To find an approximate answer.

even number   Any number divisible by two.

expanded form   Expressing a number by showing the sum of the digits times the place value of each digit.

exponent   The number that tells how many times a base number is used as a factor.

exponential notation   Writing a number with a base and its exponent.

face   The surfaces of a solid figure.

factor(s)   Numbers which when multiplied together form a product or multiple.

Fahrenheit   U.S. standard measurement for temperature. Freezing 32°F. Boiling 212°F.

fraction   A number that represents all or part of a whole.

fraction bar   Also called the division bar.

frequency distribution   The number of times data falls within a particular classification.

gram   Metric unit of the measurement of weight.

graph   A special kind of chart. The most common are bar, line, picture, and circle.

greater than   Has larger value than. 2>1

greatest common factor   The largest factor that can be divided into two numbers.

hexagon   A six-sided polygon.

horizontal   Level to or parallel to the horizon.

improper fraction   A fraction that is greater than or equal to 1. The numerator is larger than or equal to the denominator.

input   Data entered into a calculator (computer).

International Date Line   The 180th meridian. People who cross the line going west, gain a day. People who cross going east, lose a day.

intersecting lines   Lines that cross each other.

invert   To turn around the positions of the numerator and denominator of a fraction.

isosceles triangle   A triangle that has two sides of equal length.

least common multiple   The smallest multiple that two numbers have in common.

less than   Has smaller value than. 1<2

line   A continuous set of dots that has no beginning and no end.

line graph   A graph that shows data by connecting points with lines.

line segment   The part of a line that has a beginning and an end.

liter   Metric unit of liquid or dry measurement.

minuend   The number from which another number is being subtracted in a subtraction problem.

mean   The same as the average.

median   The number located exactly in the middle of a list of numbers.

meter   Metric unit of linear (line) measurement.

Metric Chart of Prefixes

smallest	_milli_	- a unit contains 1,000
	__centi__	- a unit contains 100
	___deci___	- a unit contains 10
	____unit____	- unit (meter, liter, gram)
	_____deca_____	contains 10 units
	_____hecto_____	contains 100 units
largest	_____kilo_____	contains 1,000 units

English System of Weights and Measures

Length	Weight	Dry Measure	Liquid Measure
12 inches = 1 foot	16 ounces = 1 pound	2 cups = 1 pint	16 fl ounces = 1 pint
3 feet = 1 yard	2,000 lb = 1 ton	2 pints = 1 quart	2 cups = 1 pint
36 inches = 1 yard		8 quarts = 1 peck	2 pints = 1 quart
5,280 ft = 1 mile		4 pecks = 1 bushel	4 quarts = 1 gallon
320 rods = 1 mile			

Conversion Chart

To convert	To	Multiply by	To convert	To	Multiply by
linear measure					
centimeters	inches	.394	inches	centimeters	2.54
meters	yards	1.0936	yards	meters	.914
kilometers	miles	.62	miles	kilometers	1.609
liquid measure					
liters	quarts	1.057	quarts	liters	.946
dry measure					
liters	quarts	.908	quarts	liters	1.101
weight					
grams	ounces	.0353	ounces	grams	28.35
kilograms	pounds	2.2046	pounds	kilograms	.4536

mode The number that appears most often in a list of numbers.

mixed number A number that combines a whole number and a fraction.

multiple A multiple of a number is a product of that number.

multiplicand The number being multiplied in a multiplication problem.

multiplier The number doing the multiplying in a multiplication problem.

negative number A number with a value less than zero.

norm A standard for a particular group.

number line A line with even spaces used to represent certain values.

numeral   A figure that stands for or represents a number.

numerator   The top number of a fraction. This number represents the parts being described.

obtuse angle An angle greater than a right angle (90 degrees) but less than a straight line (180 degrees).

octagon   An eight-sided polygon.

odd number Any number that cannot be divided by two.

ordered pairs   Two numbers written in a particular order so that one can be considered the first number and the other the second number.

ordinal numbers   Numbers that show position. 1st, 2nd, 3rd, 4th.....

output   The answer to data entered into a calculator (computer).

oval   A flattened circle - egg shaped.

parallel lines   Lines that are always the same distance apart.

pattern   A set arrangement or design of forms, colors, or numbers.

pentagon   A five-sided polygon.

percent   The relationship between a part and a whole. The whole is always 100.

perimeter   The distance around the outside of a closed figure.

perpendicular lines   Lines that form right or 90 degree angles.

pictograph   A graph that uses pictures to represent data.

pi (π)   3.14   Used to solve for the circumference or area of a circle.

place value   The value of a digit determined by its position in a number.

plane shape A flat shape. A plane shape is two-dimensional.

point of intersection   The one and only point that intersecting lines have in common.

polygon   A closed plane figure with three or more sides.

positive number   A number with a value greater than zero.

prediction   To tell something in advance.

prime factorization   Prime factors of a number expressed in exponential notation.

prime meridian   The longitudinal meridian (0 degrees) that passes through Greenwich, England.

prime number   A number divisible by only 1 and itself.

probability   The study of the likelihood of events.

product   The answer to a multiplication problem.

proper fraction   A fraction greater than 0 but less than 1. The numerator is smaller than the denominator.

property of zero   In addition, any number added to zero will have itself as an answer. In multiplication, any number multiplied by zero will have zero as an answer.

proportion   An equation stating that two ratios are equal.

protractor   A semi-circular instrument marked in degrees used to find the measure of an angle.

pyramid   A solid figure with a polygon as a base and triangular faces that meet at a point.

quadrilateral   A four-sided polygon.

quotient   The answer to a division problem.

radius   The distance from the center of a circle to the edge of a circle. The radius is half of the diameter.

random sample   A sample in which every member of a large group has an equal chance of being chosen.

ratio   The relationship of two numbers to each other written 1:2 or $\frac{1}{2}$.

ray   A line with one end point.

reciprocal   The fraction that results from inverting a fraction.

rectangle   A four-sided polygon with four right angles.

rectangular solid   A solid figure with six rectangular faces.

reduced fraction   A fraction equivalent to another fraction that has been written in smaller numbers. This is also called simplifying a fraction or reducing to lowest terms.

remainder   The amount that remains when a division problem has been completed.

right angle   An angle that measures 90 degrees.

right triangle   A triangle with one right angle.

Roman numerals   The ancient Roman numeral system.

I = 1   V = 5   X = 10   L = 50   C = 100   D = 500   M = 1,000

scalene triangle   A triangle with no equal sides.

sequence   Numbers arranged in a certain pattern.

similar   Figures that have the same shape but not necessarily the same size.

solid shape   A shape that takes up space. A solid shape is three-dimensional.

sphere   A geometric solid in a round shape.

square   A rectangle with all sides equal.

straight angle   An angle that measures 180 degrees.

subtrahend   The number being taken away or subtracted in a subtraction problem.

symmetry   Shapes with equal halves.

sum   The answer to an addition problem.

triangle   A three-sided polygon.

vertex   The point at which two rays or line segments meet.

vertical   Straight up and down. Perpendicular to the horizon.

volume   The measurement of space that a solid figure occupies. $V = l \times w \times h$

whole numbers   Digits arranged to represent a value equal to or greater than a whole.

Materials/ Manipulatives Needed for LIFEPAC

Chart of numbers from LIFEPAC page 4

Fact cards for addition and subtraction through 18

Counters for ones, tens, and hundreds - these may be cardboard strips 2 inches by 5 inches each set (ones, tens, hundreds) a different color. (Popsicle sticks work well as counters. Cereal boxes are an excellent source of cardboard.) pages 8 and 15.

Ten digit cards - ten pieces of cardboard 2 inches by 5 inches numbered 0 through 9 - page 13

12 inch ruler, yardstick - page 19

Digital clock, dial clock for student use, current calendar - pages 26 and 27

Objectives

1. I can remember addition and subtraction facts.
2. I can learn the meaning of digits.
3. I can count and read numbers to 999.
4. I know place value for ones, tens, and hundreds.
5. I can learn the names of addition and subtraction problems.
6. I can add and subtract on the number line.
7. I can add and subtract three-digit numbers and carry in addition to tens' place.
8. I can measure inches, feet, yards, and dozen.
9. I know operation symbols $+, -, =, \neq, >, <$.
10. I know cardinal and ordinal numbers.
11. I can tell time on the clock and on the calendar.
12. I can read and write about the things I have learned.

Teacher Notes

Part I: Addition and Subtraction Facts to 18, Numbers to 100, Digits

1. Page 1 - Have the students write their names. Discuss *Memory Verse* and *Objectives*.
2. Pages 2 and 3 - These pages contain a random selection of addition and subtraction facts. An assessment of the students' mastery of facts should be made. Students should be drilled regularly on facts not committed to memory.
3. Page 4 - Review counting to *100*. When the page is completed have the students cut out and paste or glue the chart to cardboard. It will be a useful reference for future number order problems.
4. Pages 5 and 6 - Introduce the word *digit*. Use the chart from page 4 for the number order problems. Have the students read aloud the number words on page 6. Explain that the hyphen is used to join numbers in the tens' place and ones' place.
5. Complete page 7.

Part II: Place Value, Add and Subtract, Naming Problems, Number Lines

1. Pages 8 and 9 - Use the counters to illustrate tens and ones. Explain the role of zero as a place holder. Introduce place value (3 tens = 30, 5 ones = 5). Discuss why a number is greater when the larger of two digits is in the tens' place.
2. Pages 10 and 11 - Introduce the names for addition and subtraction problems. A good mathematics vocabulary helps in explaining mathematics operations to the

students. Emphasize moving from right (ones' place) to left (tens' place) in addition and subtraction so that students will be using correct steps when they begin carrying in addition and borrowing (regrouping) in subtraction.

3. Page 12 - Use the number line to introduce addition and subtraction of multi-number problems. Although the number line is useful to introduce the concept, students should learn to complete these problems by thinking the answer.

4. Page 13 - The exercise on page 13 stresses digit location and place value. If the digit symbol cards 3 and 7 are drawn, the largest number possible is 73 and the smallest number is 37. Some digits may be drawn several times.

5. Complete page 14.

Part III: Numbers to 999, Add and Subtract, Standard Measurements

1. Pages 15 and 16 - Use the chart of numbers to introduce number order to 999. Have the students practice counting by adding one hundred, two hundred, three hundred, and so on to the numbers on the chart. Point out to the students that numbers are arranged in number order beginning with the largest place value (hundreds), looking to the next place value (tens), and finally to the last place value (ones). In the last exercise on page 15, discuss with the students why the largest digit should be in the hundreds' place and the smallest in the ones' place. Use counters to help in the explanation. Continue using counters on page 16.

2. Pages 17 and 18 - Review names of problems. Introduce addition and subtraction to hundreds' place. When adding three numbers on page 17, be sure students are adding $6 + 4 = 10$, $10 + 5 = 15$ and not counting $6 + 4 = 10$, $10 + 1 + 1 + 1 + 1 + 1 = 15$.

3. Pages 19 and 20 - Introduce standard measurements to the students. Students should have access to each one of the items listed at the bottom of the page. They should decide which measurer (12 inch ruler or yardstick) is most appropriate to use and then complete the measurement. Be sure that students are labeling answers correctly. On page 20, problems about 2, 3, and 4 dozen can be completed using addition. Students should begin committing standard measurements to memory. They may refer to page 6 to complete the number word exercises.

4. Complete page 21.

Part IV: Operation Symbols, Add with carrying, Cardinal/Ordinal Numbers, Time

1. Page 22 - This is a review page. Students should be familiar with the operation symbols. Remind them that the open side of the greater than, less than (>, <) symbols is always toward the larger number. Students may select any number for the last exercise (>, <) to make the sentence true.

2. Page 23 - Have the students read the problems, write them in digits in the corresponding boxes, and then find the answer. Monitor the students closely to be sure they are reading the number words correctly and are lining up the digits in correct place value columns. Have them name the parts of the problems when they have completed the addition and subtraction.

3. Page 24 - Students should be familiar with carrying in addition. Review the steps and have them complete the page.

4. Page 25 - Review cardinal (counting) and ordinal (order) numbers. Have the students complete the exercise writing number words (first, *not* 1st).

5. Pages 26 and 27 - Have both a digital and dial clock available for comparison. Allow the students to move the hands on the dial clock as they complete the

exercises. Have the students use a current calendar to answer questions on page 27. Keep a dial clock and current calendar on display in the classroom and use them regularly. Students should commit standard measurements to memory.

6. Complete page 28.

Part V: Review, Story Problems

1. Pages 29, 30, 31, 32, and 33 - These pages give the students an opportunity to practice the skills taught in this LIFEPAC. Questions are not grouped in any particular order and each question may deal with a different skill. Some problems will need to be written out on the LIFEPAC pages or scrap paper. Students should be allowed to read and solve the problems as independently as possible; however, they should be monitored closely so they understand this type of exercise and do not become mired in a particular problem. Students not reading at grade level may need some additional support. The teacher may use this as a test of the students' skill mastery and review concepts as needed before administering the LIFEPAC test.

2. Complete Page 34.

Administer the LIFEPAC test.

The test may be administered in two sessions. Give no help except with directions. Evaluate the tests and review areas where the students have done poorly. Review the pages and activities that stress the concepts tested.

Mathematics 302 Teacher Notes

Materials/ Manipulatives Needed for LIFEPAC

Chart of numbers showing numbers from *0* to *100* for number order exercises

Fact cards for addition and subtraction through *18*

Counters for ones, tens, and hundreds - these may be cardboard strips 2 inches by *5* inches - each set a different color. (Popsicle sticks work well as counters. Cereal boxes are an excellent source of cardboard.)

Ruler - pages 22 and 23

Pennies, nickels, dimes, quarters, dollars (play money) - page 24

Objectives

1. I know fact families.
2. I can recognize patterns.
3. I can add with carrying to hundreds' place.
4. I can skip-count by 2's, 5's, and 10's.
5. I know even and odd numbers.
6. I can read and write fractions.
7. I can learn the names of fractions.
8. I can subtract with borrowing to tens' place.
9. I can recognize flat and solid shapes.
10. I can learn about lines and end points.
11. I know pennies, nickels, dimes, quarters, and dollars.
12. I can check addition and subtraction problems.

Teacher Notes

Part I: Fact Families, Patterns, Add with carrying, Subtraction

1. Page 1 - Have the students write their names. Discuss *Memory Verse* and *Objectives*.
2. Pages 2 and 3 - Review fact families. Use several additional illustrations before assigning page 2. Explain to the children that learning is easier when they are able to recognize patterns. Be sure they understand the pattern in each exercise, page 3.
3. Pages 4, 5, and 6 - Review addition and subtraction. On page 5, review addition with carrying to tens' place.
4. Complete page 7.

Part II: Place Value, Add with carrying, Skip-count, Number Words

1. Pages 8 and 9 - Review digits, place value, and zero as a place holder.
2. Pages 10 and 11 - Introduce addition with carrying to tens' place and hundreds' place. Review addends and sum.
3. Page 12 - Introduce skip-counting by *10's, 5's,* and *2's.*
4. Page 13 - Review mental addition and subtraction and number words.
5. Complete page 14.

Part III: Even and Odd, Fractions, Subtract with borrowing

1. Page 15 - Introduce even and odd numbers. Practice addition with carrying.
2. Pages 16 and 17 - Explain to the students that a fraction represents part of a whole. A whole may be one apple, or a whole may be one set (a box) of cookies. Introduce the names for fractions - numerator, denominator, and fraction bar. Emphasize the

need for developing a good mathematics vocabulary. Be sure the students are reading and writing the fractions correctly in words.

3. Page 18 - Introduce subtraction with borrowing from tens' place (regrouping). Students who are having difficulty should use counters. Have them make a set of *7* tens' counters and *2* ones' counters. Ask if they can take *9* ones' counters from *2* ones' counters. When they answer no, tell them to convert *1* tens' counter to *10* ones' counters. Have them show they now have *6* tens' counters and *12* ones' counters. Point to the numbers *6* and *12* written in the boxes in the illustration on page 18. Ask them if they can subtract *9* from *12*. Have the students complete the subtraction problems. Continue to use the counters as needed until the students understand the process.

4. Pages 19 and 20 - Review number order and how to arrange numbers from small to large and large to small. Review the meaning of operation symbols. Review number words.

5. Complete page 21.

Part IV: Shapes, Lines, Money, Check Addition and Subtraction

1. Pages 22 and 23 - Students should know the names of shapes and be able to identify flat and solid shapes. Introduce end points. Be sure students use rulers to connect the end points on page 22. Proper use of rulers should begin early to establish good work habits for the upper grade levels.

2. Page 24 - Have a supply of coins available for the students. Have them identify each one and their relative value to each other (25 pennies = 5 nickels = 1 quarter). Explain to the students that counting pennies is counting by ones, nickels is counting by fives, dimes is counting by tens. Have them count several sets of pennies, nickels, and dimes and then combine groups of coins for counting. Explain the value of one dollar in pennies, nickels, dimes, and quarters. Work with the students to complete this page. In the last exercise, they should express the money, first in coins, and then in a combination of dollars and coins.

3. Page 25 - Review subtraction with borrowing (regrouping).

4. Pages 26 and 27 - Introduce checking addition problems. Problems that require carrying may be rewritten to allow the students to show the carry number. Introduce checking subtraction problems. Work with the students to show them where to place the carry number as they add the subtrahend to the difference in the last row of problems.

5. Complete page 28.

Part V: Review, Story Problems

1. Pages 29, 30, 31, 32, and 33 - These pages give the students an opportunity to practice the skills taught in this LIFEPAC or in the previous LIFEPAC. Questions are not grouped in any particular order and each question may deal with a different skill. Some problems will need to be written out on the LIFEPAC pages or scrap paper. Students should be allowed to read and solve the problems as independently as possible; however, they should be monitored closely so they understand this type of exercise and do not become mired in a particular problem. Students not reading at grade level may need some additional support. The teacher may use this as a test of the students' skill mastery and review concepts as needed

before administering the LIFEPAC test. Students who do poorly on page 33 need additional drill time with their fact cards.

2.   Complete page 34.

Administer the LIFEPAC test.

The test may be administered in two sessions. Give no help except with directions.

Evaluate the tests and review areas where the students have done poorly.

Review the pages and activities that stress the concepts tested.

If necessary, administer the Alternate LIFEPAC test.

Materials/ Manipulatives Needed for LIFEPAC

Chart of numbers showing numbers from *0* to *100* for number order exercises

Fact cards for addition and subtraction through *18*

Counters for ones, tens, and hundreds

Pennies, nickels, dimes, quarters, dollars (play money) - page 6

Scale(s) to measure ounces and pounds, an eraser, a cracker, a book, a box of cereal, a bag of flour, a carton of juice or milk - page 8

Standard measurers for cup, pint, quart, gallon (cup or pint should show ounces), rice, beans, dry cereal, or water - page 9

Construction paper - two pieces - page 22

Dial clock for student use - page 26

Objectives

1. I can add three numbers with carrying to tens' place.
2. I can change coins to money.
3. I can measure weight and volume.
4. I can learn more about fact families.
5. I can subtract with borrowing to hundreds' place.
6. I can skip count by 3's.
7. I can follow oral instructions.
8. I can learn about fractions equal to one whole.
9. I know the meanings of A.M. and P.M., midnight and noon.

Teacher Notes

Part I: Addition and Subtraction Facts, Add with carrying, Money

1. Page 1 - Have the students write their names. Discuss *Memory Verse* and *Objectives*.
2. Page 2 - Review fact families, addition and subtraction facts.
3. Pages 3, 4 and 5 - Review names of addition problems and addition with carrying. Introduce addition of three 2-digit numbers with carrying. On page 5, students should be able to decide whether they will need to carry by looking at the ones' and tens' places. If they estimate a 2-digit answer, they know they will need to carry. Instruct them to be careful about placing the carry number directly above the column it is being carried to.
4. Page 6 - Practice reading number words. There are nine banks at the bottom of the page. Each bank has a total of *50¢*, *$1.00*, or *$1.50* in coins. Have the students convert the coins to money and then color the bank the corresponding color.
5. Complete page 7.

Part II: Measurements, Fact Families, Place Value, Check Addition

1. Pages 8 and 9 - It is very important that students use a hands on approach when studying measurements. Have the listed materials available for each lesson. Review standard measurements for length and time introduced in LIFEPAC 301.

   | 12 inches = 1 foot | 36 inches = 1 yard | 3 feet = 1 yard | 12 units = 1 dozen |

   60 minutes = 1 hour   24 hours = 1 day

   7 days = 1 week   30 or 31 days = 1 month   365 days = 1 year

   On pages 8 and 9, students learn the standard measurements for weight and volume. They should individually take part in each exercise. On page 9, use rice, beans, or dry cereal to measure. The exercises may be expanded using additional examples as available in the school or home. Students should commit standard measurements to memory.

2. Page 10 - Introduce fact families when zero is one of the numbers.

3. Page 11 - In the second exercise remind students that, if they have three digits, they are able to write six different numbers. Discuss with them the change in value for each digit when it is moved from ones' place to tens' place to hundreds' place. Discuss the use of zero as a place holder.

4. Pages 12 and 13 - Review addition with carrying and checking answers. Monitor the students closely and correct errors as soon as possible. Students are reinforcing incorrect procedures each time they use them.

5. Complete page 14.

Part III: Subtract with borrowing, Check Subtraction, Number Sentences, Oral Instruction

1. Pages 15 and 16 - Review names of subtraction problems. Review subtraction problems. Introduce subtraction with borrowing from the hundreds' place.

2. Page 17 - Each of the first set of problems should be written in digits and operation symbols. For example, the answer to the first problem is written $73 > 68$. Review the symbols with the students before assigning the page.

3. Page 18 - Use objects for counting to introduce skip-counting by 3's.

4. Page 19 - Review checking subtraction problems.

5. Page 20 - Dictation develops the students' ability to follow oral instruction.

> *Listen and write.* Dictate:
>
> yellow heart - Write the number words (spelling and hyphen must be correct) - eleven, forty-seven, five hundred thirty-two, four hundred six
>
> green heart - Write number sentences in digits and symbols -
>
> $$8 + 3 = 9 + 2, \quad 146 > 142, \quad 8 \neq 13 - 4, \quad 2 + 3 < 10 - 4$$
>
> blue heart - Start at 73. Write the missing numbers to 63.
>
> orange heart - Draw a picture of a gallon container. Show how full it would be if it contained a quart of orange juice.
>
> pink heart - Draw (measure) 2 inches.
>
> purple heart - Draw a dial clock with the time 4:43. Write the time.
>
> red heart - Write the fractions 1/3, 2/5, 5/8, 7/9. Draw an illustration of one of the fractions. (Example: Divide a circle into 3 parts and color 1 part.)

6. Complete page 21.

> *Listen and write.* Dictate:
>
> green heart - Write the fractions 7/8, 3/5, 1/2.
>
> purple heart - Draw a dial clock with the time 7:18. Write the time.

Part IV: Fractions, Addition, Time, Place Value

1. Pages 22 and 23 - Follow instructions carefully. Students need as much opportunity as possible to develop an understanding of fractions. On page 22, instruct students to glue the parts of the cut-out rectangle onto the rectangle drawn on paper in such a way that all four parts will fit.

2. Pages 24 and 25 - Review addition with carrying - no carry boxes.
3. Page 26 - Point out the positions of the sun in relation to the clocks. Talk about a day meaning a *24* hour period *or* the period of time that it is light. Discuss when an official day begins and ends (midnight to midnight). Talk about the hour hand and the minute hand. When we say the clock goes around twice, is it the hour hand or the minute hand that goes around twice? Talk about A.M. and P.M.
4. Page 27 - Review place value.
5. Complete page 28.

Part V: Review, Story Problems

1. Pages 29, 30, 31, 32, and 33 - These pages give the students an opportunity to practice the skills taught in this LIFEPAC or in previous LIFEPACs. Questions are not grouped in any particular order and each question may deal with a different skill. Some problems will need to be written out on the LIFEPAC pages or scrap paper. Students should be allowed to read and solve the problems as independently as possible; however, they should be monitored closely so they understand this type of exercise and do not become mired in a particular problem. Students not reading at grade level may need some additional support. The teacher may use this as a test of the students' skill mastery and review concepts as needed before administering the LIFEPAC test.
2. Complete page 34.

Administer the LIFEPAC test.

The test may be administered in two sessions. Give no help except with directions.
Evaluate the tests and review areas where the students have done poorly.
Review the pages and activities that stress the concepts tested.
If necessary, administer the Alternate LIFEPAC test.

Materials/ Manipulatives Needed for LIFEPAC

Chart of numbers showing numbers from *0* to *100* for number order exercises
Fact cards for addition and subtraction through *18*
Counters for ones, tens, hundreds, and thousands
Current calendar - page 12
Pennies, nickels, dimes, quarters, dollars (play money) - page 18
Construction paper, scissors - pages 24 and 25

Objectives

1. I can read and write numbers to thousands' place.
2. I can learn place value to thousands' place.
3. I can round numbers to tens' place.
4. I can estimate in addition using rounded numbers.
5. I can subtract with borrowing from both
   tens' place and hundreds' place.
6. I can measure to the half-inch and quarter-inch.
7. I can solve horizontal addition and subtraction problems.
8. I can learn about Roman and Arabic numerals.
9. I can add and subtract fractions.

Teacher Notes

Part I: Numbers to Thousands' Place, Addition

1. Page 1 - Have the students write their names. Discuss *Memory Verse* and *Objectives*.
2. Pages 2 and 3 - Introduce thousands' place. Point out the comma. Caution students not to use the word *and* when reading whole numbers.
3. Pages 4, 5, and 6 - Review addition. Introduce addition with *3* numbers, *3*-digits, no carrying. Some problems will result in answers to the thousands' place. Remind students to use commas in these answers. Review place value, skip-counting, even and odd numbers.
4. Complete page 7.

Part II: Rounding, Estimation, Subtract with Borrowing, Quarter-inch

1. Pages 8 and 9 - Rounding numbers is the basis for estimation. To solve a problem mentally (paper, pencil, calculator not available), students need to know whether they have a reasonable answer. Estimation tells them if their answer is reasonable.
2. Pages 10 and 11 - Be sure students understand borrowing (regrouping) from tens' place and hundreds' place. Page 11 introduces borrowing from both places.
3. Pages 12 and 13 - Each student should have a current calendar and ruler to be able to independently answer the questions on these pages. Students may need some discussion on the seasons. They may enjoy making drawings of their favorite activities of the month.
4. Complete page 14.

Part III: Number Words, Place Value, Add and Subtract

1. Page 15 - Review facts and fact families. Continue regular drilling on facts.
2. Page 16 - Students are introduced to number words to thousands' place.

Emphasize comma, hyphen, and correct spelling.

3. Page 17 - Introduce place value to the thousands' place.
4. Pages 18 and 19 - Review number order, standard measurements, fractions as words, money, patterns, operation symbols. Use the chart of numbers for number order problems. Actual coins may be helpful in converting money to coins.
5. Page 20 - Introduce horizontal and vertical addition and subtraction. Monitor the students' work to be sure they are writing numbers correctly in place columns. It may be helpful to show the first example with the 2 and 7 incorrectly placed in the hundreds' and tens' columns and the resulting incorrect sum. Compare this to the sum when the numbers are lined up correctly.
6. Complete page 21.

Part IV: Roman Numerals, Count by 3's, Add and Subtract Fractions
1. Page 22 - Introduce Roman numerals. Review plane and solid shapes.
2. Page 23 - Review counting by 3's. Skip-counting is the basic introduction to the multiplication tables. Multiplication will be introduced in a later LIFEPAC.
3. Pages 24 and 25 - These exercises are meant to help the students understand addition and subtraction of fractions. If the students are having difficulty with the concept (adding or subtracting just the numerators), have them cut a rectangle from paper and divide it into 6 equal parts. Work through the addition and subtraction problems in the examples. Continue using this procedure for the exercises on pages 24 and 25 as helpful. In the exercise using the set of hearts, begin with nine hearts in the set so the students understand the denominator of 9. Have them select 4 hearts and describe them as 4/9 and 3 hearts described as 3/9. Or, on page 25, it would be 6 hearts described as 6/9 and 2 hearts described as 2/9.
4. Pages 26 and 27 - Review addition and subtraction.
5. Complete page 28.

Part V: Review, Story Problems
1. Pages 29, 30, 31, 32, and 33 - These pages give the students an opportunity to practice the skills taught in this LIFEPAC or in previous LIFEPACs. Questions are not grouped in any particular order and each question may deal with a different skill. Some problems will need to be written out on the LIFEPAC pages or scrap paper. Students should be allowed to read and solve the problems as independently as possible; however, they should be monitored closely so they understand this type of exercise and do not become mired in a particular problem. Students not reading at grade level may need some additional support. The teacher may use this as a test of the students' skill mastery and review concepts as needed before administering the LIFEPAC test. Page 33 - Dictation develops the students' ability to follow oral instruction.

Listen and write. Dictate:

First ball - Write the numbers after   27,   198,   503,   2,758.
              Write the numbers before   53,   60,   249,   3,680.
Second ball - Write the next six numbers in sequence after 967.

Third ball -   Write the numbers in place value columns.

356	27	840	4,386
24	182	607	581
7	36	211	2,883

Fourth ball - Write the numbers on the lines. Then, arrange them in number order.

3,286   2,386   8,326   6,623   2,836   8,263

Fifth ball -   Write in number words.

five thousand, two hundred sixty-three

four thousand, eight hundred five

2. Complete page 34.

Administer the LIFEPAC test.

The test may be administered in two sessions. Give no help except with directions.

Evaluate the tests and review areas where the students have done poorly.

Review the pages and activities that stress the concepts tested.

If necessary, administer the Alternate LIFEPAC test.

Materials/ Manipulatives Needed for LIFEPAC

Chart of numbers showing numbers from *0* to *100* for number order exercises

Fact cards for addition and subtraction through *18*

Counters for ones, tens, hundreds, thousands

Fahrenheit thermometer, a cup of ice water, a cup of tap water, a cup of hot water (as hot as it is safe for student to handle), ruler, and crayons - page 10

Ruler, crayons, paper, scissors - page 15

Ruler, table knife, fork, spoon, square inch made from paper, a piece of construction paper 6 inches by 4 inches - page 18

Pennies, nickels, dimes, quarters, dollars (play money) - page 30

Objectives

1. I can name whole numbers and fractions.
2. I can write number sentences.
3. I can expand numbers to thousands' place.
4. I can read a Fahrenheit thermometer.
5. I can collect data and post it to a bar graph.
6. I can draw lines of symmetry.
7. I can round numbers to hundreds' place.
8. I can estimate in addition using rounded numbers.
9. I can learn about linear and square inches.
10. I can measure perimeter.
11. I can learn rules for adding even and odd numbers.

Teacher Notes

Part I: Number Sentences, Add and Subtract, Ordinal Numbers, Fractions

1. Page 1 - Have the students write their names. Discuss *Memory Verse* and *Objectives*.
2. Pages 2 and 3 - Review numbers to the thousands' place. Point out that the comma makes the number easier to read, because it separates the thousands' place from the other numbers. Have the students say the thousands' number, and then continue reading the number as if it were simply a hundreds' number. If *0* is in the hundreds' place or tens' place, do not say that place.
3. Page 4 - Review addition, subtraction of whole numbers, and names of problems.
4. Page 5 - Extend the concept of ordinal numbers to ninety-ninth.
5. Page 6 - Review addition, subtraction of fractions, and names of problems.
6. Complete page 7.

Part II: Place Value, Add and Subtract, Temperature, Graphs

1. Page 8 - Introduce place value to thousands. First, have the children identify 'how many' in each place and then, convert 'how many' to place value. Emphasize that the value of the digit changes if it changes its place in the number.
2. Page 9 - Introduce addition of three numbers, 3-digits. There are no carry boxes. Monitor students carefully to be sure the carry number is going above the correct column. The exercise at the bottom of the page brings students one step closer to multiplication tables for 2's, 5's, and 3's.

3. Pages 10 and 11 - It is essential for students' to use a hands-on approach to these pages. On page 11, the question 'Did the temperature go up or down ...' assumes the thermometer is in an upright position when being read. Most students should be familiar with the bar graph. Have the students write in - indoor, outdoor, hand, ice water, tap water, and hot water - on the lines along the left side of the graph. Tell them to draw a line on the graph that shows the temperature for each listed item and then color to that point.

4. Page 12 - Review number words and operation signs.

5. Page 13 - Review steps to borrow from both tens' place and hundreds' place. It is usually less confusing for students if they complete the borrowing and regrouping before actually subtracting the numbers. Students having difficulty should continue to use counters to illustrate the problems.

6. Complete page 14.

Part III: Plane Shapes, Symmetry, Rounding, Estimation, Perimeter

1. Page 15 - Introduce new shapes of pentagon, hexagon, and octagon. Introduce the meaning of lines of symmetry.

2. Pages 16 and 17 - Introduce rounding to hundreds' place. Students should begin to understand that rounding to the hundreds' place only requires them to look at tens' place. If the number is less than 5, they round down. If the number is 5 or more, they round up. Have the students round the numbers, complete the addition, and compare answers. Emphasize the value of rounding in helping them arrive at a sensible answer.

3. Pages 18 and 19 - Students have learned that inches are standard measurements. The inch that they have learned about should be further defined as a linear inch. Introduce the square inch. Be sure that students have the materials required for this lesson and that each student completes each exercise individually. Students tend to misunderstand the concept of perimeter and area measurement. They must have a good mental image of linear and square shapes. Keep their square inches with their rulers as a reminder. On page 19, introduce perimeter. Stress the fact that perimeter measures lines and so we use linear measurement.

4. Page 20 - The students are required to rewrite the horizontal problems as vertical problems. They should be monitored carefully. Incorrect columns will automatically result in an incorrect answer. The second exercise on page 20 may be done orally: *6 plus 3 equals 9, 9 minus 2 equals 7, 7 plus 8 equals 15,* and so on.

5. Complete page 21.

Part IV: Rules for Even and Odd, Roman Numerals, Checking Addition and Subtraction

1. Page 22 - Learning the rules for even and odd in addition and subtraction is another way for students to identify whether they do or do not have a sensible answer.

2. Page 23 -Review plane shapes, perimeter, and lines of symmetry. Have the students complete the matching exercise and write the numbers in number order.

3. Pages 24 and 25 - Review checking addition and subtraction problems. Checking becomes more difficult as the numbers become larger due to carrying, borrowing,

and regrouping. Students who write neatly and place numbers where they belong will have the most success.

4. Page 26 - Review the values of Roman numerals and Arabic numerals. Introduce the correct placement of Roman numerals for fours and nines. Review digits and operation symbols.

5. Page 27 - Be sure students are following the correct steps to complete fraction problems. Have them use paper cutouts (rectangles divided into 5, 8, 2, ... parts) to illustrate some of the problems. Have them read the problems aloud after they are completed. (Three-fifths plus one-fifth equals four-fifths.)

6. Complete page 28.

Part V: Review, Story Problems

1. Pages 29, 30, 31, 32, and 33 - These pages give the students an opportunity to practice the skills taught in this LIFEPAC or in previous LIFEPACs. Questions are not grouped in any particular order and each question may deal with a different skill. Some problems will need to be written out on the LIFEPAC pages or scrap paper. Students should be allowed to read and solve the problems as independently as possible; however, they should be monitored closely so they understand this type of exercise and do not become mired in a particular problem. Students not reading at grade level may need some additional support. The teacher may use this as a test of the students' skill mastery and review concepts as needed before administering the LIFEPAC test.

2. Complete page 34.

Administer the LIFEPAC test.

The test may be administered in two sessions. Give no help except with directions. Evaluate the tests and review areas where the students have done poorly.

Review the pages and activities that stress the concepts tested.

If necessary, administer the Alternate LIFEPAC test.

Materials/ Manipulatives Needed for LIFEPAC

Chart of numbers showing numbers from *0* to *100* for number order exercises
Fact cards for addition and subtraction through *18*
Counters for ones, tens, hundreds, thousands
Dial clock with second hand, suitable for student use - page 6
Large piece of paper, ruler, yardstick, large table - page 10
Construction paper, ruler, scissors, buttons - pages 16 and 17
Pennies, nickels, dimes, quarters, dollars (play money) - page 18
Crayons and ruler - page 24

Objectives

1. I can add and subtract numbers to thousands.
2. I can learn the multiples for 2, 3, 5, and 10.
3. I can learn the meaning of 'quarter after' and 'quarter til'.
4. I can learn to give sensible answers.
5. I can learn to measure perimeter and area.
6. I can learn about equivalent fractions.
7. I can add and subtract money using dollar and cent signs.
8. I can learn the operation sign for multiplication.
9. I can learn multiplication facts for 2.
10. I can learn about line graphs.
11. I can learn about line segments and angles.

Teacher Notes

Part I: Addition, Multiples, Time

1. Page 1 - Have the students write their names. Discuss *Memory Verse* and *Objectives*.
2. Pages 2 and 3 - Review names of addition problems. Introduce addition to thousands' place with and without carrying.
3. Page 4 - Review skip-counting. Introduce multiples. Review ordinal numbers.
4. Page 5 - The pattern of even and odd numbers as answers to addition problems helps students identify a correct or incorrect answer.
5. Page 6 - Students should recognize the term *standard measurements*. A dial clock is recommended for this page to help students identify the hands on the clock and to understand the meanings of "quarter after" and "quarter til."
6. Complete page 7.

Part II: Subtraction, Sensible Answers, Measurements, Fractions

1. Page 8 - Review names of subtraction problems. Introduce subtraction to thousands' place without borrowing.
2. Page 9 - Be sure the students do not miss the object of the lesson. Always check answers to be sure they are sensible.
3. Pages 10 and 11 - Students have difficulty with the concept of linear measurement and square measurement, perimeter and area. It is essential that the directions are followed exactly as presented on these pages. Students may not want to write all of the numbers on the square foot, but do have them count to *144* and write the number *144* on the final square inch. Keep the square foot for future use. Glue it

to a cardboard backing. Have the students use it to measure additional flat surfaces. Have them make a square yard by laying out nine square feet. Take them for a drive so they grasp the concept of a linear mile and a square mile.

4. Page 12 - Review names of fraction problems, addition and subtraction of fractions. Point out that fraction problems can be written as horizontal or vertical problems. They are easier to solve when rewritten as vertical problems. (This is important for students as they learn to solve problems with unlike denominators.)

5. Page 13 - Review place value, zero as a place holder, and operation signs. Point out that the largest numbers are written with digits in descending order. The smallest numbers are written with digits in ascending order.

6. Complete page 14.

Part III: Add and Subtract, Fractions, Money

1. Page 15 - Review addition and number words.

2. Pages 16 and 17 - These pages introduce the concept of equivalent fractions. Allow the students to use construction paper and scissors to draw and cut out the rectangles on page 16. Begin by having the students cut the first rectangle into two parts and write the fraction 1/2. Have the students divide the rectangle into four parts. Point out that two of the four parts (2/4) is the same as (equal to) one of two parts (1/2). Have them write the fraction 2/4. Continue in this manner to complete the page. On page 17, divide a set of eight buttons into two groups of 4. The students will probably recognize four buttons as one-half a set. Have them write 1/2. Now divide the set into four groups of two. Point out to the students that there are now four groups, so the denominator of the fraction is four. Have them write the four. Set aside two of the groups and tell them that the two groups represent the numerator. Tell them to complete the fraction 2/4. Point out that the same number of buttons (4) represents one-half (1/2) and two-fourths (2/4). Complete the page in this manner. Continue this type of exercise using various shapes and sets. This a difficult concept for students. They will need to work with it many times before they understand it.

3. Page 18 - Review money signs. Point out the one dollar bill and the five dollar bill. Monitor the students' work carefully.

4. Pages 19 and 20 - Review Roman numerals, rounding, subtraction, and facts.

5. Complete page 21.

Part IV: Multiplication, Bar and Line Graphs, Line Segments, Angles

1. Page 22 - Introduce multiplication, multiplication sign (x), and multiples of 2.

2. Page 23 - Have the students write the colors on the left side of the bar graph and then complete the graph. Introduce line graphs.

3. Page 24 - Review lines and end points. Introduce line segments and angles. The object of this lesson is to familiarize students with terms used in geometry. Be sure they use rulers to connect end points.

4. Pages 25, 26, and 27 - Review facts, temperature, operation symbols, number order, number words, multiples of 2, addition, and subtraction.

5. Complete page 28.

Part V: Review, Story Problems

1. Pages 29, 30, 31, 32, and 33 - These pages give the students an opportunity to

practice the skills taught in this LIFEPAC or in previous LIFEPACs. Questions are not grouped in any particular order and each question may deal with a different skill. Some problems will need to be written out on the LIFEPAC pages or scrap paper. Students should be allowed to read and solve the problems as independently as possible; however, they should be monitored closely so they understand this type of exercise and do not become mired in a particular problem. Students not reading at grade level may need some additional support. The teacher may use this as a test of the students' skill mastery and review concepts as needed before administering the LIFEPAC test. On page 32, discuss with the students that the days in the month vary; and that every four years (leap year), there is an extra day in the year.

2. Complete Page 34.

Administer the LIFEPAC test.

The test may be administered in two sessions. Give no help except with directions.

Evaluate the tests and review areas where the students have done poorly.

Review the pages and activities that stress the concepts tested.

If necessary, administer the Alternate LIFEPAC test.

Materials/ Manipulatives Needed for LIFEPAC

Chart of numbers showing numbers from *0* to *100* for number order exercises

Fact cards for addition and subtraction through *18*

Fact cards for multiplication for *2's* and *5's* - page 5

Counters for ones, tens, hundreds, and thousands

Objects for counting - page 5

10 cards approximately *2* inches by *3* inches in size - one side should be blank - the other side should be marked or colored in some way with color markers or crayons - *4* cards - green, *3* cards - yellow, *2* cards - orange, *1* card blue - also crayons - page 16

Crayons and ruler - pages 32 and 33

Objectives

1. I can learn the meaning of multi-digit numbers.
2. I can subtract numbers to thousands' with borrowing.
3. I can learn multiplication facts for 5.
4. I can read and write mixed numbers.
5. I can add and subtract mixed numbers.
6. I can learn to subtract with zeros in the minuend.
7. I can learn rules for subtracting even and odd numbers.
8. I can learn the value of knowing probability.
9. I can learn about circle graphs.
10. I can find missing numbers in addition problems.

Teacher Notes:

Part I: Add and Subtract, Multiplication Facts, Mixed Numbers

1. Page 1 - Have the students write their names. Discuss *Memory Verse* and *Objectives*.
2. Pages 2, 3, and 4 - Review the meaning of digits, addition and subtraction of four-digit numbers with carrying and borrowing.
3. Page 5 - Have the students write multiples of numbers through times (x) 10. When the page is complete introduce objects for counting. Ask the students to tell you the value of 3 sets of 2, 6 sets of 2, and so on. Tell them to illustrate the problem and the answer. Do this with a variety of facts for *2's* and *5's*. Introduce the fact cards.
4. Page 6 - Introduce mixed numbers.
5. Complete page 7.

Part II: Measurements, Subtraction, Mixed Numbers, Even and Odd, Probability

1. Pages 8 and 9 - Students should have mastered standard measurements for time, weight, and volume. They should understand the relationship between linear and square measurements and know the standard measurements for linear and square units. They should understand that perimeter is measured in linear units and area in square units and that answers must be labeled using correct terms.
2. Page 10 - Introduce borrowing when there is a zero in the minuend. Students will be more accurate in their work if they complete the regrouping process before doing the actual subtraction.
3. Page 11 - Introduce addition and subtraction of mixed numbers.
4. Page 12 - Students can apply the even and odd rule to subtraction.

5. Page 13 - The study of probability is a very important concept in mathematics. Students should develop a good understanding of the meaning of probability and be comfortable using the term. They should understand the relationship between probability and patterns.

6. Complete page 14.

Part III: Probability, Graphs, Solid Shapes

1. Page 15 - Review place value, operation signs, number order, Roman numerals. Students have learned to change Roman numerals to Arabic numerals. To change Arabic to Roman, reverse the steps. Follow the example.

2. Pages 16 and 17 - Introduce the circle on page 16 as a circle graph. Point out to the students that information is much easier to understand when it is shown in a graph (bar, line, circle). Discuss the meaning of probability. Probability promotes logical thinking. Probability guides us in certain directions when solving problems in mathematics and in other subjects. Ask the students why there is a greater probability of turning up the color green than the color blue. Be sure the students mix the ten cards thoroughly each time before making their selections. Discuss their selections and compare them with the probabilities.

3. Page 18 - Review numbers and number words, facts, missing number problems.

4. Page 19 - Review addition and subtraction.

5. Page 20 - Review lines of symmetry, flat and solid shapes. Introduce the term *face*. The sides of many solid shapes have the appearance of flat shapes. The sides of the solid shapes are called *faces*.

6. Complete page 21.

Part IV: Money, Missing Number Problems, Rounding, Estimation

1. Page 22 - Review coin and cents equivalents. Review fact families.

2. Page 23 - Many of the students will want to approach these problems simply as problems in subtraction; however, missing number problems lay the foundation for setting up algebraic equations. Have the students follow the steps exactly as shown.

3. Page 24 - Students should learn that there are two ways to check an addition problem. Using subtraction to check a problem lays the groundwork for additional missing number problems.

4. Page 25 - Introduce estimation of subtraction problems by rounding numbers.

5. Page 26 - Students should have a sufficient grasp of the steps in subtraction so that they no longer need the boxes for borrowing and regrouping. Impress on them the importance of neat work and keeping numbers in columns. The boxes have been a clue to them as to when borrowing was and was not necessary. They will need to make that decision on their own when the boxes are no longer in the problems.

6. Page 27 - Review multiplication facts for 2's and 5's. Students should have addition and subtraction facts committed to memory. Regular drill of multiplication facts is appropriate now.

7. Complete page 28.

Part V: Review, Story Problems

1. Pages 29, 30, 31, 32, and 33 - These pages give the students an opportunity to practice the skills taught in this LIFEPAC or in previous LIFEPACs. Questions are

not grouped in any particular order and each question may deal with a different skill. Some problems will need to be written out on the LIFEPAC pages or scrap paper. Students should be allowed to read and solve the problems as independently as possible; however, they should be monitored closely so they understand this type of exercise and do not become mired in a particular problem. Students not reading at grade level may need some additional support. The teacher may use this as a test of the students' skill mastery and review concepts as needed before administering the LIFEPAC test. Page 32 continues the study of equivalent fractions. Have the children divide the plane shape into 5 parts, the diamond into 4 parts, the sets into groups of 6 and 3. The students should then be able to identify the denominator and from that point be able to find the numerator of the fraction. Page 33, the students may use the colors as shown to color the bar and circle graphs.

2. Complete Page 34.

Administer the LIFEPAC test.

The test may be administered in two sessions. Give no help except with directions.

Evaluate the tests and review areas where the students have done poorly.

Review the pages and activities that stress the concepts tested.

If necessary, administer the Alternate LIFEPAC test.

Mathematics 308 Teacher Notes

Materials/ Manipulatives Needed for LIFEPAC

Chart of numbers showing numbers from *0* to *100* for number order exercises
Fact cards for addition and subtraction through *18*
Fact cards for multiplication for 2's, 3's, 5's, 10's - page 22
Counters for ones, tens, hundreds, and thousands
Current calendar - page 6
Pennies, nickels, dimes, quarters, dollars (play money) - page 12
6 inch ruler - page 16
Crayons - pages 32 and 34

Objectives

1. I can express measurements in more than one unit.
2. I can find the missing addend and check the answer.
3. I can learn about decimal numbers.
4. I can subtract with zeros in the minuend.
5. I can learn to give change in money problems.
6. I can learn more about adding mixed numbers.
7. I can learn directions-north, south, east, west.
8. I can learn about picture graphs.
9. I can learn multiplication facts for 3 and 10.
10. I can learn the multiples of 4.
11. I can learn about length and width.

Teacher Notes

Part I: Shapes, Measurements, Add, Subtract

1. Page 1 - Have the students write their names. Discuss *Memory Verse* and *Objectives*.
2. Pages 2 and 3 - Review plane and solid shapes, standard measurements.
3. Pages 4 and 5 - Review checking addition by adding up and adding down. Introduce checking by subtracting an addend from the sum. Use this method to teach solving for a missing number (addend).
4. Page 6 - Review the calendar, number order to *9,999*, and mental arithmetic.
5. Complete page 7.

Part II: Decimals, Subtraction, Making Change

1. Page 8 - Review fractions, whole numbers, mixed numbers, and rules for even, odd.
2. Page 9 - Introduce decimals written as *.1* through *.9* (one tenth - nine tenths). Do not expect too much of the students. The objective is to add the word *decimal* to their vocabulary as it is used somewhere other than in money and to learn that there is a correlation between decimals and fractions.
3. Pages 10 and 11 - Review the steps for subtraction with *0* and borrowing carefully. Students who are neat in their work will be rewarded with correct answers.
4. Page 12 - Students may need actual money (play) to complete exercises.
5. Page 13 - Review multiplication facts, number words, rounding and estimation. Emphasize to students - problems in the tens should be rounded to tens, problems in hundreds should be rounded to hundreds.
6. Complete page 14.

Part III: Number Order, Mixed Numbers, Directions - N,S,E,W, Graphs

1. Page 15 - Review place value, number order, number words to thousands.
2. Pages 16 and 17 - Use the ruler to help clarify the meanings of fraction, whole number, and mixed number. *Follow directions carefully.* Students must use their own rulers to measure on the ruler on page 16. Use other manipulatives to teach the concept of a fraction equal to one whole. Cut a paper circle into four parts. Have the students write a fraction for one part, two parts, three parts, and four parts. (Do not confuse them by trying to add *1/4* to *1/2*. Most students are not ready to learn about common denominators.)
3. Pages 18 and 19 - Students should be familiar with maps and the directions of north, south, east, west. Explain to the students that this is another form of standard measurement. Directions always stay the same. Have the students start at *Go* and find the numbers on the chart. *2 E/2 S* means to begin at *Go*, move two spaces east, and two spaces south (4). When the students have completed page 18 by finding the answers to the facts, have them gather the data by answering the questions at the top of page 19. The picture graph is the last of the four main types of graphs that the students will learn about.
4. Page 20 - Review addition and subtraction. Students who do not know their addition and subtraction facts need regular drill.
5. Complete page 21.

Part IV: Multiplication, Length and Width, Fractions, Add and Subtract

1. Page 22 - Introduce students to multiples of *3* and *10*, to the facts for *3* and *10*, and to the fact cards for *3* and *10*. Students who have mastered addition and subtraction facts may begin drilling on multiplication facts.
2. Page 23 - Introduce the terms *length* and *width* as they apply to a rectangle. Point out to students that they can solve for the perimeter if they know the measurements for length and width. Review addition of mixed numbers. Have students convert fractions in their answers to the whole number *1* and add to the other whole numbers in the problem. Have them identify the final answer as a fraction, whole number, or mixed number.
3. Page 24 - Review equivalent fractions. Use other manipulatives to help present this concept. Cut a rectangle into *9* parts. *1/3 = 3/9* Cut into *8* parts. *1/2 = 2/4 = 4/8* Cut into *10* parts. *1/2 = 5/10*
4. Pages 25, 26, and 27 - Review operation signs, Roman numerals, place value, addition and subtraction. Students are provided work space to rewrite horizontal problems.
5. Complete page 28.

Part V: Review, Story Problems

1. Pages 29, 30, 31, 32, and 33 - These pages give the students an opportunity to practice the skills taught in this LIFEPAC or in previous LIFEPACs. Questions are not grouped in any particular order and each question may deal with a different skill. Some problems will need to be written out on the LIFEPAC pages or scrap paper. Students should be allowed to read and solve the problems as independently as possible; however, they should be monitored closely so they understand this type of exercise and do not become mired in a particular problem.

Students not reading at grade level may need some additional support. The teacher may use this as a test of the students' skill mastery and review concepts as needed before administering the LIFEPAC test. Page 32, the students may use the colors as shown to color the bar and circle graphs.

2. Complete Page 34.

Administer the LIFEPAC test.

The test may be administered in two sessions. Give no help except with directions. Evaluate the tests and review areas where the students have done poorly.

Review the pages and activities that stress the concepts tested.

If necessary, administer the Alternate LIFEPAC test.

Materials/ Manipulatives Needed for LIFEPAC

Chart of numbers showing numbers from *0* to *100* for number order exercises

Fact cards for addition and subtraction through *18*

Fact cards for multiplication for *2's, 3's, 4's, 5's, 10's*

Counters for ones, tens, hundreds, and thousands

Objects for counting

Thermometer showing Fahrenheit and Celsius degrees - page 10

Grocery store items that show liters or grams - page 25

Crayons - page 33

Objectives

1. I can add and subtract whole numbers to thousands.
2. I can add and subtract fractions and whole numbers.
3. I know standard measurements for time, length, weight, volume, directions, and temperature.
4. I can learn metric units for temperature, weight, and volume.
5. I can read bar, line, picture, and circle graphs.
6. I know multiplication facts for 2, 3, 4, 5, and 10.
7. I know place value to thousands.
8. I know operation symbols for +, -, =, ≠, >, <, x.

Teacher Notes

Part I: Add and Subtract Whole Numbers, Read Fractions and Mixed Numbers

1. Page 1 - Have the students write their names. Discuss *Memory Verse* and *Objectives*.
2. Pages 2 and 3 - Review addition and subtraction facts, lines of symmetry, terms used with sizes and shapes.
3. Pages 4 and 5 - Review number words for fractions and mixed numbers, standard measurements for time, fact families, and digits.
4. Page 6 - Students should understand that a fraction represents a relationship between two numbers. Three parts of a set of three (3/3), four parts of a set of four (4/4) are both equal to one whole. Use objects for counting or other manipulatives to help the students in understanding this concept.
5. Complete page 7.

Part II: Measurements, Operation Signs, Add Fractions and Mixed Numbers.

1. Pages 8 and 9 - Review checking addition and subtraction problems. Review even and odd, operation symbols > , <, and time to the minute.
2. Pages 10 and 11 - Students will need to have an understanding of the metric system. It is appearing more frequently in the United States and is widely used in foreign countries. Have the students become familiar with the term Celsius but do not expect them to learn the standard measurements. At this point, the students will simply confuse them with the other standard measurements they are expected to know. Continue review of operation symbols =, ≠, +, −, x, directions, and plane shapes.
3. Page 12 - Students should now have a good grasp of fractions that are equal to one whole. When they add fractions, they should learn to convert these fractions to one (4/4 = 1) as part of their answer. For students having difficulty, cut out 8 circles

from cardboard. Divide one circle into *9* parts. Illustrate *5 4/9 + 2 2/9 = 7 6/9*. Use the same method to show *4 2/5 + 2 3/5 = 7* wholes.

4. Page 13 - Review length, width, perimeter, bar graph, and calendars.
5. Complete page 14.

Part III: Measurements, Multiplication Facts, Number Order, Number Words, Graphs

1. Pages 15, 16, and 17 - Review line graph, solid shapes, and missing numbers. Remind students that they can find the missing number by totaling the addends and subtracting from the sum. Review digital time, multiplication facts for *2, 5,* and *10,* coins, and standard measurements for linear and square measurement.
2. Pages 18 and 19 - Students practice subtraction of fractions and mixed numbers. Review picture graph, multiplication facts for *3* and *4.*
3. Page 20 - Review place value and number words.
4. Complete page 21.

Part IV: Rounding, Metrics, Fractions

1. Page 22 - Review standard measurements for weight and dozen, mental arithmetic, operation symbols. Discuss the last exercise - horizontal addition - with the students. Emphasize to them that the numbers must be written in the correct place value columns.
2. Page 23 - Introduce rounding to thousands' place.
3. Page 24 - Remind students that they should always try for a logical answer when solving mathematics problems.
4. Page 25 - Review standard measurements for volume. Continue the introduction of metric units that was begun on page 10. Talk about liters for volume and grams for weight and compare to the English Standard of Measurements. Do not expect too much of the students. They are simply adding these words to their vocabulary.
5. Page 26 - This is another opportunity for students to understand that fractions show a relationship between two numbers. One-half can be equal to two-fourths, one-third can be equal to two-sixths. Review circle graphs.
6. Page 27 - Review Roman and Arabic numerals. Monitor the students work closely. Be sure they are writing the subtraction problems in correct place value columns.
7. Complete page 28.

Part V: Review, Story Problems

1. Pages 29, 30, 31, 32, and 33 - These pages give the students an opportunity to practice the skills taught in this LIFEPAC or in previous LIFEPACs. Questions are not grouped in any particular order and each question may deal with a different skill. Some problems will need to be written out on the LIFEPAC pages or scrap paper. Students should be allowed to read and solve the problems as independently as possible; however, they should be monitored closely so they understand this type of exercise and do not become mired in a particular problem. Students not reading at grade level may need some additional support. The teacher may use this as a test of the students' skill mastery and review concepts as needed before administering the LIFEPAC test.
2. Complete Page 34.

Administer the LIFEPAC test.

The test may be administered in two sessions. Give no help except with directions.

Evaluate the tests and review areas where the students have done poorly.

Review the pages and activities that stress the concepts tested.

If necessary, administer the Alternate LIFEPAC test.

Materials/ Manipulatives Needed for LIFEPAC
> Chart of numbers showing numbers from *0* to *100* for number order exercises
> Fact cards for addition and subtraction through *18*
> Fact cards for multiplication for *2's, 3's, 4's, 5's, 10's*
> Counters for ones, tens, hundreds, and thousands
> Objects for counting
> Circles from construction paper the size of the bottle caps. Draw pictures or write the names of fish on the circles as follows: *5* goldfish, *4* tuna, *2* dolphins, *1* shark. Glue the circles inside *12* bottle caps. Also needed - a plastic or metal container safe for student use as a fish bowl - page 10
> Eight *1* inch squares made from paper or cardboard - page 31

Objectives
> 1. I can round numbers to thousands' place.
> 2. I can estimate addition and subtraction problems to thousands' place.
> 3. I can add and subtract fractions vertically and horizontally.
> 4. I can learn more about probability.
> 5. I can learn about equations.
> 6. I can learn to make two sides of a problem equal to each other.
> 7. I can learn to use parentheses in two-step problems.
> 8. I can study the relationship between perimeter and area measurement.

Teacher Notes
> **Part I: Rounding, Add and Subtract, Whole Numbers, Fractions**
> 1. Page 1 - Have the students write their names. Discuss *Memory Verse* and *Objectives*.
> 2. Pages 2 and 3 - Round numbers and estimate answers for *10's, 100's,* and *1,000's*.
> 3. Pages 4 and 5 - Practice addition and subtraction of whole numbers and fractions.
> 4. Page 6 - Review multiples, fact families, and standard measurements for time.
> 5. Complete page 7.
> **Part II: Ordinal Numbers, Even and Odd, Probability, Multiplication Facts**
> 1. Pages 8 and 9 - Review ordinal numbers, standard measurements (linear and square), mental arithmetic, even and odd, fractions as words.
> 2. Pages 10 and 11 - Use the bottle caps prepared for the lesson. The study of probabilities teaches students to predict what may happen based on facts or data they have gathered. It promotes logical thinking. On page 11, the students should draw from the fish bowl twelve times. There should be twelve bottle caps in the bowl each time the student draws. The object of the lesson is to find out how close the students will come to the probabilities.
> 3. Pages 12 and 13 - Review checking addition and subtraction problems. Practice multiplication facts for *2's, 3's, 4's, 5's,* and *10's*.
> 4. Complete page 14.

Part III: Fractions, Number Order, Measurements, Missing Numbers

1. Page 15 - Review fractions equal to *1* whole. Review standard measurements for weight and dozen.
2. Page 16 - Reintroduce decimal fractions to tenths. Review number order to thousands. Remind students that it is easy to write the largest or smallest numbers. Simply arrange the digits in order of descending or ascending value.
3. Page 17 - Review addition and subtraction of fractions and mixed numbers. Review standard measurements for volume.
4. Page 18 - Complete number sentences. Review area and perimeter. Have students draw in the square measurements.
5. Page 19 - Reintroduce method for finding a missing number in addition and subtraction problems.
6. Page 20 - Review number words to thousands. Convert coins to money.
7. Complete page 21.

Part IV: Time, Flat and Solid Shapes, Patterns, Place Value

1. Pages 22 and 23 - Review time, rounding, standard measurements, flat and solid shapes, lines of symmetry.
2. Pages 24 and 25 - Review patterns, Arabic and Roman numerals, place value.
3. Page 26 - Practice addition and subtraction.
4. Page 27 - Each number sentence on this page represents a complete problem. The object is to monitor the students' ability to read and understand fractions written in words. Problems should be written vertically. Allow the students to work as independently as possible.
5. Complete page 28.

Part V: Review, Story Problems

1. Pages 29 and 30 - Page 29 introduces the concept of equations. An equation is a number sentence that shows two sets of values equal to each other. Use objects for counting for students who have difficulty solving the problems. Students should show two ways to make the sides of the equation equal. Page 30 introduces problems using parentheses.
2. Page 31 - This exercise develops the students spatial concepts. It also reinforces the students' understanding of perimeter and area measurements.
3. Pages 32 and 33 - These pages give the students an opportunity to read and apply skills taught in this LIFEPAC or in previous LIFEPACs.
4. Complete Page 34.

Administer the LIFEPAC test.

   The test may be administered in two sessions. Give no help except with directions.
   Evaluate the tests and review areas where the students have done poorly.
   Review the pages and activities that stress the concepts tested.
   If necessary, administer the Alternate LIFEPAC test.

ADDITIONAL ACTIVITIES

1. Plan **regular drill** periods for **mathematics facts**. These should occasionally be timed. They may be either oral or written.

2. **Manipulatives, hand-held objects**, are basic to developing a relationship between the written problem and an understanding by the student of the problem solution. Manipulatives are both appropriate and essential at all grade levels. A majority of the manipulatives used in problems may be developed from material already available in the classroom or home. Measurements require measuring cups, rulers, and empty containers. Boxes and other similar items help the study of solid shapes. Construction paper, beads, buttons, beans are readily available to use for counting, fractions, sets, grouping, sequencing, and flat and solid shapes. **Manipulatives may extend to drawings.** For example, students may draw the shape of a figure when solving for area or perimeter. Have the students use colored pencil or crayons to show the figure's dimensions and flat surface. Then have them explain the logic of their answers.

3. **Dictation** strengthens comprehension. Dictate problems with answers for students to write on paper. (Five plus six equals eleven or 5 + 6 = 11.) This will help them to develop vocabulary and spelling of mathematics terms. Problems may be written numerically or in words.

4. Keep a **log book of terms** with which the student is having difficulty. These may be identified from the *Introduction of Skills* or the *Mathematics Terms*. Quiz the student regularly until the term is mastered.

5. An **oral arithmetic bee** can be held in which problems are given orally and must be solved mentally. Selected LIFEPAC pages may be used for this exercise. Teach estimation and grouping of numbers for easier problem solving.

6. The student may create **number patterns** for others to solve.

When studying geometry,

7. Create 2- and 3-dimensional figures out of construction paper or cardboard.

8. Create figures that are congruent and/or similar. Form circles, squares, and rectangles from triangles. Try making octagons and pentagons from triangles, squares and rectangles. Cut figures into geometric shapes similar to jigsaw puzzles and then put back together.

When studying measurements,

9. Use groups of coins to show what combination of coins may be worth a certain amount of money.

10. Using local newspaper advertisements, have students make a collage of the items they could buy if they had $10.00 to spend. Prices should be included on the clippings.

11. Have students fill containers and then use a combination of measurers such as cup and quart, ounce and pound to determine quantity and weight.

12. Have the students measure their height, length of arms, legs and feet, the lengths around their heads, arms, wrists, and ankles.

When studying statistics,

13. Gather data to form charts and graphs. Begin with gathering the data; then, decide how the data could be most effectively presented. Suggestions for data collection would be number of people living in each home, students' eye color, shoe size, height, weight, food preferences.

14. LIFEPAC **word problems** often reflect everyday experiences of the student. If a problem relates to the distance, rate and time of travel when a family visits friends or relatives, develop a similar problem the next time an actual trip is taken. Use all possible opportunities to translate word problems into similar real experiences.

T

E

S

T

S

Reproducible Tests
for use with the Mathematics
300 Teacher's Guide

MATHEMATICS

3 0 1

ALTERNATE

LIFEPAC TEST

$\frac{40}{50}$

Name _____

Date _____

Score _____

MATHEMATICS 301: Alternate LIFEPAC TEST

1. **Write the ten digits.** (5 points)

_____ _____ _____ _____ _____ _____ _____ _____ _____ _____

2. **Write the number words.**

703 _____

961 _____

3. **Write the numbers in number order.** (4 points)

72   17   600   38   931   430   204   3

_____ _____ _____ _____ _____ _____ _____ _____

4. **Write how many.** Write the value. (4 points)

86 = _____ tens + _____ ones   276 = ____ hundreds + ____ tens + ___ ones

86 = _____ + _____ .   276 = _____ + _____ + _____

5. **Find the answers.** Name the problem.

difference   subtrahend   addend   sum   minuend

34   _____   59   _____

+ 62   _____   − 36   _____

_____ _____   _____ _____

6. **Think the answer.** Write the answer.

$4 + 3 + 8 - 9 =$ _____ $13 - 8 + 6 + 8 =$ _____

74

7. **Add or subtract.**

```
  37          4          56         423        459        865
+  5          3        + 47       + 259       − 32       − 132
            + 9
```

8. **How many ...**   inches in a foot? _____   inches in a yard? _____

9. **Write the answer on the line.**   yards   inches   dozen   feet

What would you use to measure ...

how tall you are? _____   the size of a pencil? _____

10. **Write the sentences using digits and operation symbols.**

Five plus four is equal to nine.   _____

Seven minus three is not equal to five.   _____

11. **Circle the operation sign.**

6 + 4 (=, ≠) 2 + 8   12 − 5 (=, ≠) 11 − 5

4 + 8 (>, <) 18 − 9   16 − 7 (>, <) 9 + 8

12. **Write the ordinal number word.**

63   24   46   59   73   18

Forty-six is the _____ number in the row.

Seventy-three is the _____ number in the row.

13. **Write the answer.**

How many
days in a week? _____

_____ : _____

75

14. Add or subtract.

437 + 61 = _____   325 + 360 = _____   748 − 307 = _____

15. Read the story. Work the problem.   (2 points)

Betsy and John were collecting rocks.
Betsy had 23 rocks. John had 35 rocks.
How many rocks did they have altogether?   _____

Betsy and John decided to share
18 of their rocks with James.
How many rocks do Betsy and John have now?   _____

MATHEMATICS

302

ALTERNATE

LIFEPAC TEST

Name_____

Date _____

Score _____

MATHEMATICS 302: Alternate LIFEPAC TEST

1. **Complete the fact family.**   6, 7, 13   (2 points)

    _____ _____ = _____   _____ _____ = _____

    _____ _____ = _____   _____ _____ = _____

2. **Write the next two numbers in the number pattern.**
    Circle even or odd.   (2 points)

    3, 5, 7, 9, _____, _____, ...   even odd

3. **Add or subtract.**

    ```
      6        578       683       876        ☐☐        ☐☐
      4      + 49      +249      - 351        72        43
    + 7                                     - 56      - 28
    ```

4. **Write the value of the underlined digit.**

    5̲67 _____   Zero is a _____.

5. **Write how many.** Write the value.   (2 points)

    804 = _____ hundreds + _____ tens + _____ ones

    804 = _____ + _____ + _____.

6. **Write the problem.** Find the answer.   (4 points)

    The minuend is 75 and   The addends are
    the subtrahend is 57.   632 and 151.
    What is the difference?   What is the sum?

7. Write the answer. (4 points)
When we count by ...

10's, the numbers end in _____. 5's, the numbers end in _____ or _____.

2's, the numbers end in _____, _____, _____, _____, or _____.

8. Write the number words.

13 _____   380 _____

9. Write the names.
fraction bar denominator numerator

$$\frac{1\ \rule{2cm}{0.4pt}}{4\ \rule{2cm}{0.4pt}}$$

_____

10. Draw a picture of the fraction $\frac{3}{5}$.

11. Write the fraction in words $\frac{3}{7}$. _____

12. Circle the symbol.

9 − 5 (>, <) 3 + 7   423 (>, <) 432

7 + 6 (=, ≠) 15 − 7   8 + 0 (=, ≠) 8 − 0

13. Follow directions. Write the answers.   (4 points)
Connect the end points. A, B   B, C   C, A

Name the shape. _____

Is this a flat or solid shape? _____

A curved line that is closed may be called a _____.

A
•

•   •
C   B

14. Write the words.

3 + 6 ≠ 12 _____

18 − 9 > 7 _____

79

15. Write the amount of coins ...   in cents.   in dollars and cents.

_____   _____

16. Add and subtract. Check answers.   (4 points)

$$\begin{array}{r} 236 \\ + \ 421 \\ \hline \end{array}$$ $$\begin{array}{r} 529 \\ + \ 250 \\ \hline \end{array}$$ $$\begin{array}{r} 87 \\ - \ 42 \\ \hline \\ + \\ \hline \end{array}$$ $$\begin{array}{r} 64 \\ - \ 43 \\ \hline \\ + \\ \hline \end{array}$$

17. Write the standard measurements.

_____ inches = 1 foot   _____ inches = 1 yard   _____ feet = 1 yard

18. Read the story. Work the problem.   (2 points)

Ben was at the bakery in the grocery store. He counted 23 chocolate doughnuts and 13 sugar doughnuts. How many doughnuts did he count altogether?

_____

Ben's mother said he could buy a dozen chocolate doughnuts and 4 sugar doughnuts. How many chocolate and sugar doughnuts were left at the bakery?

_____

MATHEMATICS

303

ALTERNATE LIFEPAC TEST

40 / 50

Name _____

Date _____

Score _____

MATHEMATICS 303: Alternate LIFEPAC TEST

1. **Write the fact families.** (4 points)

7, 0, 7 _____   _____   _____   _____

16, 8, 8 _____   _____   _____   _____

2. **Name the problem.** (6 points)

difference   addend   minuend   sum   subtrahend

$$58$$
$$+ 76$$ _____
$$\overline{134}$$ _____

$$95$$
$$- 53$$ _____
$$\overline{42}$$ _____

3. **Write the number words in digits.**

eight hundred six   _____

4. **Add and subtract.**

87	366	470	□□ 93	□□ 384	□□ 639
+ 59	+ 285	+ 250	− 46	− 127	− 284

5. **Write the standard measurements.**

_____ ounces = 1 pound   _____ pounds = 1 ton

_____ ounces = 1 pint   _____ cups = 1 pint

_____ pints = 1 quart   _____ quarts = 1 gallon

6. **Write the standard measurement that you would use to measure ...**

milk for cereal. _____   how much you weigh. _____

7. **Write the largest and smallest number.**

3, 6, 1   largest _____   smallest _____

8. **Add and subtract. Check.**

```
     543              259            □□              □□
   + 261            + 386            93             652
                                   − 46            − 137

                                  +               +
```

9. **Write sentences.** Use digits and operation symbols.   (2 points each)

Jeremy completed 4 math pages on Monday
    and 2 on Tuesday. Jodie completed
    4 pages on Monday and 3 on Tuesday.
    Show that the number of pages that
    Jeremy completed are not equal to the
    number of pages that Jodie completed.   _____

Chris has six people in his family. Linda has
    four people in her family. Compare the
    number of people in Chris's family
    to the number of people in Linda's family.   _____

10. **Write the fractions in digits.**

two-eighths _____   five-ninths _____

11. **Write the fraction that represents the shaded part.**

_____   _____

12. **Write the fraction that describes...**

the whole rectangle. _____   the whole set of toys. _____

13. Write the answer.

What time of day does it change from Tuesday to Wednesday? _____

The clock shows noon. What will the time be after 12 hours? _____

Mark usually eats breakfast at 7:30 _____. (A.M., P.M.)

14. Write the place of the underlined digit. Write the value.

8<u>3</u>4 _____ _____

15. Count the coins. Write the money.

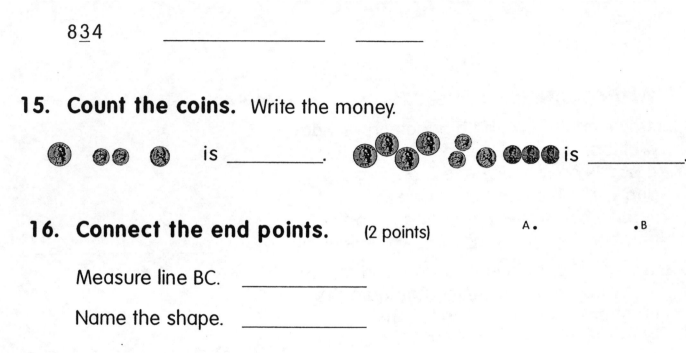

_____ is _____.   _____ is _____.

16. Connect the end points. (2 points)

Measure line BC. _____

Name the shape. _____

A•   •B

D•   •C

MATHEMATICS

ALTERNATE
LIFEPAC TEST

$$\frac{40}{50}$$

Name_____

Date _____

Score _____

MATHEMATICS 304: Alternate LIFEPAC TEST

	ones	tens	hundreds	thousands

1. **Write the place of each underlined digit.**

    4,<u>3</u>68 _____   <u>5</u>,261 _____

2. **Write the number.**
    6 in the hundreds' place, 4 in the ones' place
    5 in the thousands' place, and 7 in the tens' place.   _____

3. **Write the numbers that come after.**   (1 point)

    6,235 6,236 _____ _____ _____ _____ _____

4. **Solve the problem.** Think the answer. Write the answer.

    5 + 3 + 9 _____   8 + 6 + 5 = _____

5. **Add and subtract.**

658	547	235	☐☐	☐☐☐	☐☐☐
+ 172	+ 539	451	72	534	651
		+ 103	− 48	− 269	− 368

6. **Round each addend.** Add the rounded numbers.
    Add the problems.   (4 points)

    42   rounds to
    + 29   rounds to   + _____

7. **Measure.**

    _____   _____ inches

    _____   _____ inches

86

8. **Write the standard measurements.**

_____ feet = 1 yard   _____ cups = 1 pint   _____ months = 1 year

_____ ounces = 1 pound   _____ inches = 1 foot   _____ minutes = 1 hour

9. **Write the number word.**

6,302 _____

10. **Write how many.** Write the value. (2 points)

2,563 = _____ thousands _____ hundreds _____ tens _____ ones

2,563 = _____ + _____ + _____ + _____

11. **Write the money in dollars and coins.**
Show two examples. (2 points)

	dollars	quarters	dimes	nickels	pennies
$4.37 =	_____	_____	_____	_____	_____
=	_____	_____	_____	_____	_____

12. **Circle the correct operation symbols.**

6,163 (>, <) 6,136   8 + 3 (=, ≠) 5 + 6   4 + 2 + 5 (>, <) 13

13. **Rewrite the problems.**
Add or subtract. (2 points)

426 + 58 + 7 =

632 − 147 =

14. **Write Roman numerals in Arabic numerals.** (2 points)

XVII = X + V + I + I = _____ + _____ + _____ + _____ = _____

15. Start at 0. Count by 3's to 30. Circle the numbers. (2 points)

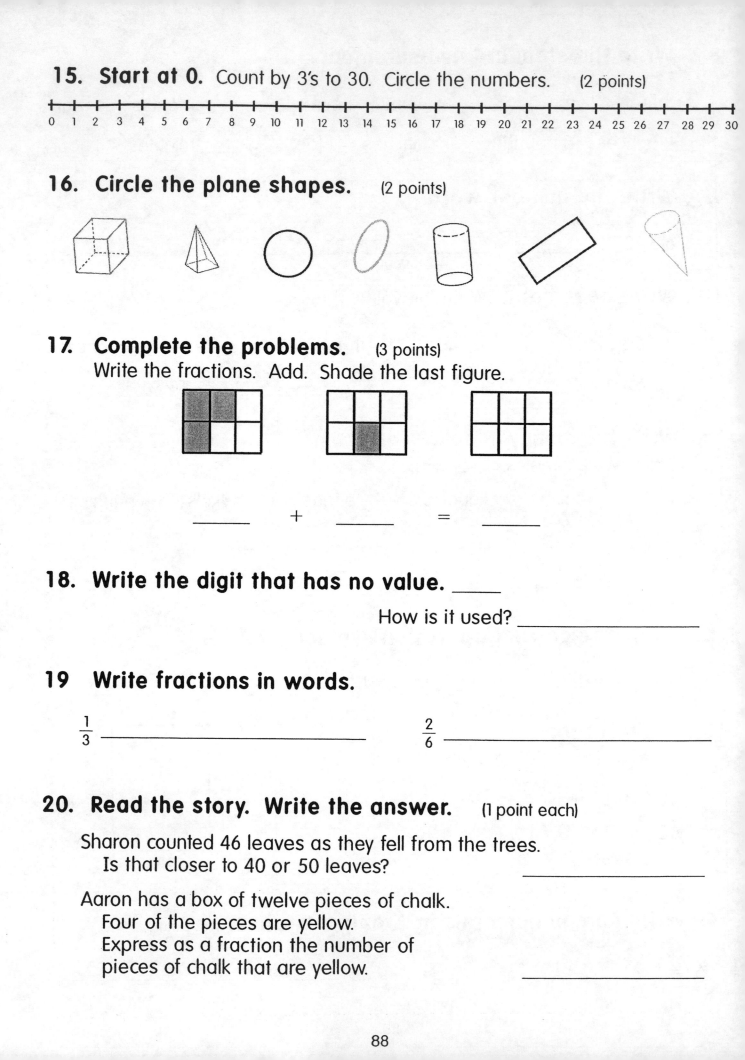

16. Circle the plane shapes. (2 points)

17. Complete the problems. (3 points)
Write the fractions. Add. Shade the last figure.

_____ + _____ = _____

18. Write the digit that has no value. _____

How is it used? _____

19 Write fractions in words.

$\frac{1}{3}$ _____ $\frac{2}{6}$ _____

20. Read the story. Write the answer. (1 point each)

Sharon counted 46 leaves as they fell from the trees.
  Is that closer to 40 or 50 leaves?

_____

Aaron has a box of twelve pieces of chalk.
  Four of the pieces are yellow.
  Express as a fraction the number of
  pieces of chalk that are yellow.

_____

MATHEMATICS

3 0 5

ALTERNATE LIFEPAC TEST

40 / 50

Name_____

Date _____

Score _____

MATHEMATICS 305: Alternate LIFEPAC TEST

1. **Write the missing commas.** Cross out numbers that do not belong. Write the correct number above. (2 points)

   6 3 2 1   6 3 2 2   6 3 3 2   6 3 2 4   6 3 5 2

2. **Circle the even numbers.** (2 points)

   36   75   108   424   763   569   252   347

3. **Read the problem in words.** Write in numbers. Add or subtract.

   Sixty-five plus thirty-seven equals _____.

   Ninety-one minus forty-six equals _____.

4. **Add or subtract.**

   378   639   935   430
   + 746   + 481   − 267   − 273

5. **Match.** (3 points)

   forty-sixth   92
   twenty-ninth   46
   sixty-third   15
   ninety-second   63
   seventy-eighth   29
   fifteenth   78

6. **Add or subtract.**

   $\frac{4}{9}$ $\frac{3}{8}$ $\frac{5}{6}$ $\frac{7}{9}$
   $+ \frac{2}{9}$ $+ \frac{2}{8}$ $- \frac{1}{6}$ $- \frac{4}{9}$

7. **Write the temperature for each form of water.**

   ice _____ degrees F.   steam _____ degrees F.

8. **Measure.**

   _____   _____ inches

9. **Show the data on the bar graph.** (4 points)

The inside temperature is 80 degrees F. and
the outside temperature is 15 degrees F.

Temperature in Degrees F.

_____

_____

0 10 20 30 40 50 60 70 80 90 100

10. **Write the number sentences in words.**

6 + 8 < 9 + 9 _____

8 − 0 = 4 + 4 _____

11. **Round each addend.** (4 points)

Add the rounded numbers. Add the problems.

373   rounds to
+ 230   rounds to   + _____

12. **Measure the perimeter.** (5 points)

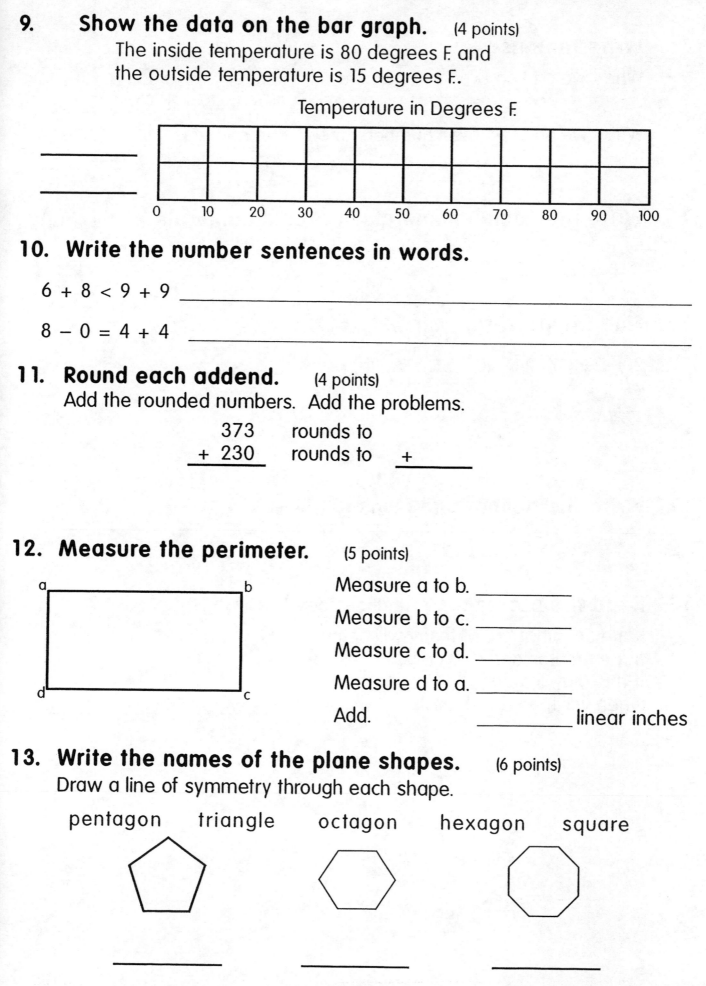

Measure a to b. _____

Measure b to c. _____

Measure c to d. _____

Measure d to a. _____

Add.   _____ linear inches

13. **Write the names of the plane shapes.** (6 points)

Draw a line of symmetry through each shape.

pentagon   triangle   octagon   hexagon   square

_____   _____   _____

14. Write the answer.

When we add an even number and odd number together,
the answer is _____.

When we add two even numbers or two odd numbers,
the answer is _____.

15. Write the Roman numerals in Arabic numerals. (2 points)

XXIV = _____ = _____ = _____

16. Find the pattern. Write what comes next.

20, 19, 17, 14, 10, ...   _____

   _____

17. Write the dollars and coins. (1 point)

$3.29   _____

18. Read the problem. Write the answer. (2 points)

Katie said that her birthday will be in
three months and four days.
If it is May 5 today,
when will it be Katie's birthday?   _____

MATHEMATICS

306

ALTERNATE

LIFEPAC TEST

$\dfrac{40}{50}$

Name _____

Date _____

Score _____

MATHEMATICS 306: Alternate LIFEPAC TEST

1. **Add or subtract.**

3,276	1,658	4,365		723	946	7,469
+ 2,105	+2,257	+2,186		− 286	− 538	− 2,248

2. **Write the multiples of 2.**   (2 points)

_____, _____, _____, _____, _____, _____, _____, _____, _____, _____

3. **Add.** Write E (even) or O (odd). Write 'yes' or 'no' for pattern. (3 points each)

               (yes, no)   (yes, no)

$35 + 22 =$ _____ $54 + 42 =$ _____

___ + ___ = ____   _____   ___ + ___ = ____   _____

4. **Write the standard measurements.**

_____ seconds = 1 minute   _____ hours = 1 day

_____ inches = 1 yard   _____ days = 1 year

_____ square inches = 1 square foot   _____ square feet = 1 square yard

5. **Write the perimeter and area measurement.**
Label answers correctly.

perimeter _____

area   _____

3 feet

3 feet

6. **Write the largest and smallest numbers.**   3 7 5 0

largest _____   smallest _____

7. Rewrite the fraction problems. Add or subtract.

$$\frac{2}{5} + \frac{1}{5} =$$

$$\frac{9}{12} - \frac{5}{12} =$$

8. Circle the correct operation signs.

4,085 (=, ≠) 4,185   6 + 8 (=, ≠) 9 + 3   5,426 (>, <) 5,264   3 + 4 (>, <) 14 − 6

9. Write the fraction for the shaded part.

_____

_____

10. Write the money in digits. Add.   (3 points)

_____

+ _____

11. Write Roman numerals in Arabic numerals.   (2 points)

LXIV = _____ = _____ = _____

12. Round the numbers. Add.   (2 points each)

65 _____

+ 83 _____

423 _____

+ 576 _____

13. Write in digits and operation signs.

Sixteen minus eight is equal to eight plus zero.   _____

Eighty-five is greater than fifty-eight.   _____

14. Complete the line graph.

Show 4 green cars, 6 blue cars, and 8 white cars.   (1 point)

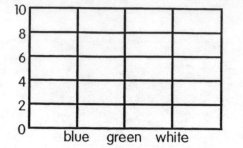

15. Draw an example of ...

an angle.

a line segment
    with end points.

16. Write the temperature.

_____ °F.

17. Write in number words.   3,061

_____

18. Find the answer to the problem.   (2 points)

Joanne had $4.50 to spend at the store. She spent $3.48 on drawing paper, and 67¢ on pencils. How much money did Joanne have after she paid for the drawing paper and the pencils?   _____

MATHEMATICS

ALTERNATE

LIFEPAC TEST

40 / 50

Name _____

Date _____

Score _____

MATHEMATICS 307: Alternate LIFEPAC TEST

1. **Write multiples.**

   $6 \times 2 =$ _____ $3 \times 2 =$ _____ $4 \times 5 =$ _____ $8 \times 5 =$ _____

2. **Write in words.**

   $\dfrac{4}{8}$ _____ $3\dfrac{1}{3}$ _____

3. **Add.**

3,574	2,179	2,844	432
+ 2,865	+ 4,856	+ 5,768	176
			+ 239

4. **Subtract.**

753	435	9,367	8,206
− 286	− 278	− 4,522	− 3,478

5. **Write the standard measurements for length and square units.**

   _____ inches = 1 foot   _____ feet = 1 mile

   _____ square inches = 1 square foot   _____ square feet = 1 square yard

6. **Find the perimeter and area.**
   Label answers.

   1 square inch

   perimeter _____   area _____

7. **Add or subtract.**

$3\dfrac{4}{7}$	$8\dfrac{7}{9}$
$+ 5\dfrac{2}{7}$	$- 6\dfrac{4}{9}$

8. Subtract. Write E (even) or O (odd) on the line below each number. Did your answer follow the pattern? Write 'yes' or 'no'. (3 points each)

(yes, no)   (yes, no)

64 – 36 = _____   72 – 39 = _____

____ – ____ = ____   _____   ____ – ____ = ____   _____

9. Write Arabic numerals in Roman numerals. (2 points)

36 = _____ = _____ = _____

84 = _____ = _____ = _____

You have 10 cards,
3 brown, 3 purple, 2 green, and 2 orange.

10. Color the graph.
Show the color of the cards.

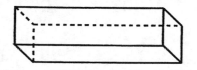

11. Write the probabilities.

The probability of selecting an brown card is _____ out of 10.

The probability of selecting an orange card is _____ out of 10.

12. Draw lines of symmetry.   **13. Color a face on the solid shape.**

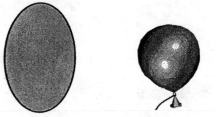

14. Read the problem. Subtract. Write the numbers on the lines. Check your answer.

Problem:

83 + _____ = 152 because 152 – 83 = _____. Subtract.

15. Write the number of cents.

2 quarters + 2 dimes – 3 pennies = _____

4 dimes – 3 nickels – 2 pennies = _____

16. Round. Add or subtract. Compare answers.   (2 points each)

$$
\begin{array}{r}
823 \\
+\ 204 \\
\hline
\end{array}
\qquad\qquad
\begin{array}{r}
78 \\
-\ 32 \\
\hline
\end{array}
$$

17. Read the problem. Solve.

Juan has collected 6 Liberty Nickels and 8 Indian Head Pennies.
Cody has collected 9 Buffalo Nickels and 6 Steel Pennies.
Which one of the boys has more coins?

Write your answer using operation symbols (>, <).   _____

Jennifer has 12 candy kisses. Corrie has 3 less candy kisses
than Jennifer. Lorie had the same number as Corrie, but she
ate 2. How many candy kisses does each one have now?

Jennifer _____   Corrie _____   Lorie _____

18. In which number does the digit 3 have the greatest value?

2,803   3,000   8,306   7,239   _____

19. Draw ...   an angle   a line segment   a curved line.

MATHEMATICS

3 0 8

ALTERNATE LIFEPAC TEST

$\dfrac{40}{50}$

Name _____

Date _____

Score _____

MATHEMATICS 308: Alternate LIFEPAC TEST

1. **Write the answer.**   faces, closed lines, angles, rectangle, squares

   Plane shapes are drawn using _____.

   _____ are formed when two lines meet at an end point.

   The sides of solid shapes are named _____.

2. **Write the measurement that is equal.**

   3 yards = _____ feet   2 pints = _____ cups

3. **Find the missing numbers.**   (2 points)

Problem	Add	Subtract	Check		Problem	Add	Subtract	Check
18					136			
29					285			
+ ?					+ ?			
63					681			

4. **4.** July is the _____ month of the year.

5. **Describe as fraction or mixed number.** Write in words.

   $\frac{6}{8}$ _____   _____

   $4\frac{2}{5}$ _____   _____

6. **Add.** Write the even or odd rule that applies.

   32 + 45 = _____   _____ + _____ = _____

7. **Write the decimal for the fraction.** Write in numbers and words.

   $\frac{3}{10}$ = _____   _____

8. Show the change.

Price	Amount Paid	Change	Dollars and Coins Paid
$3.62	$5.00	_____	_____

9. Add.

$$\begin{array}{r} 5{,}398 \\ +\ 2{,}654 \\ \hline \end{array} \qquad \begin{array}{r} 4{,}882 \\ +\ 1{,}437 \\ \hline \end{array} \qquad \begin{array}{r} 276 \\ 382 \\ +\ 565 \\ \hline \end{array} \qquad \begin{array}{r} 436 \\ 271 \\ +\ 542 \\ \hline \end{array}$$

10. Subtract.

$$\begin{array}{r} 795 \\ -\ 386 \\ \hline \end{array} \qquad \begin{array}{r} 9{,}003 \\ -\ 5{,}001 \\ \hline \end{array} \qquad \begin{array}{r} 4{,}000 \\ -\ 2{,}638 \\ \hline \end{array} \qquad \begin{array}{r} 6{,}053 \\ -\ 4{,}576 \\ \hline \end{array}$$

11. Round. Add or subtract.   (2 points each problem)

$$\begin{array}{r} 542 \\ +\ 367 \\ \hline \end{array} \quad \text{_____} \qquad\qquad \begin{array}{r} 831 \\ -\ 429 \\ \hline \end{array} \quad \text{_____}$$

12. Write numbers for the number words.

two thousand, fifty-one _____   seven thousand, four _____

13. Add mixed numbers.

$$\begin{array}{r} 6\frac{1}{3} \\ +\ 2\frac{2}{3} \\ \hline \end{array} \qquad \begin{array}{r} 5\frac{3}{8} \\ +\ 4\frac{1}{8} \\ \hline \end{array} \qquad \begin{array}{r} 4\frac{1}{2} \\ +\ 2\frac{1}{2} \\ \hline \end{array} \qquad \begin{array}{r} 7\frac{3}{9} \\ +\ 2\frac{4}{9} \\ \hline \end{array}$$

14. Draw arrows for the directions.   ←   ↑ ↓   →   (2 points)

west _____   south _____   east _____   north _____

15. Show what the students ate for breakfast on the picture graph.   (2 points)

3 ate oatmeal.
7 ate cornflakes.
6 ate pancakes.
2 ate toast.

```
_____
_____
_____
_____
         0  1  2  3  4  5  6  7  8
```

16. Write the multiples.   (2 points)

8 x 2 = _____   7 x 5 = _____   3 x 3 = _____   4 x 10 = _____

17. Circle $\frac{2}{3}$ of the set of cones.   (2 points)

How many cones is that? _____

18. Write the Arabic numerals in Roman numerals.   (2 points)

224 = _____ = _____ = _____

19. The measurement for one unit of the shape is shown.

Find the perimeter and area. Label answers correctly.

1 linear yard

perimeter _____

area   _____

20. Write the answers.   (2 points)

Kelly, Brian, and Jason had completed their spelling tests. Brian had a score of 24. Jason scored 2 points higher than Brian. Kelly scored 3 points lower than Jason. What was the score for each student?

Kelly _____   Brian _____   Jason _____

MATHEMATICS

3 0 9

ALTERNATE
LIFEPAC TEST

$$\frac{40}{50}$$

Name _____

Date _____

Score _____

MATHEMATICS 309: Alternate LIFEPAC TEST

1. **Write the answers to the facts.** (2 points)

7	8	9	2	9	14	16	12	8	7
+4	+3	+0	+5	+7	-8	-7	-9	-6	-0

2. **Draw a line of symmetry.**

3. **Match.**

line segment

curved line

perimeter

angle

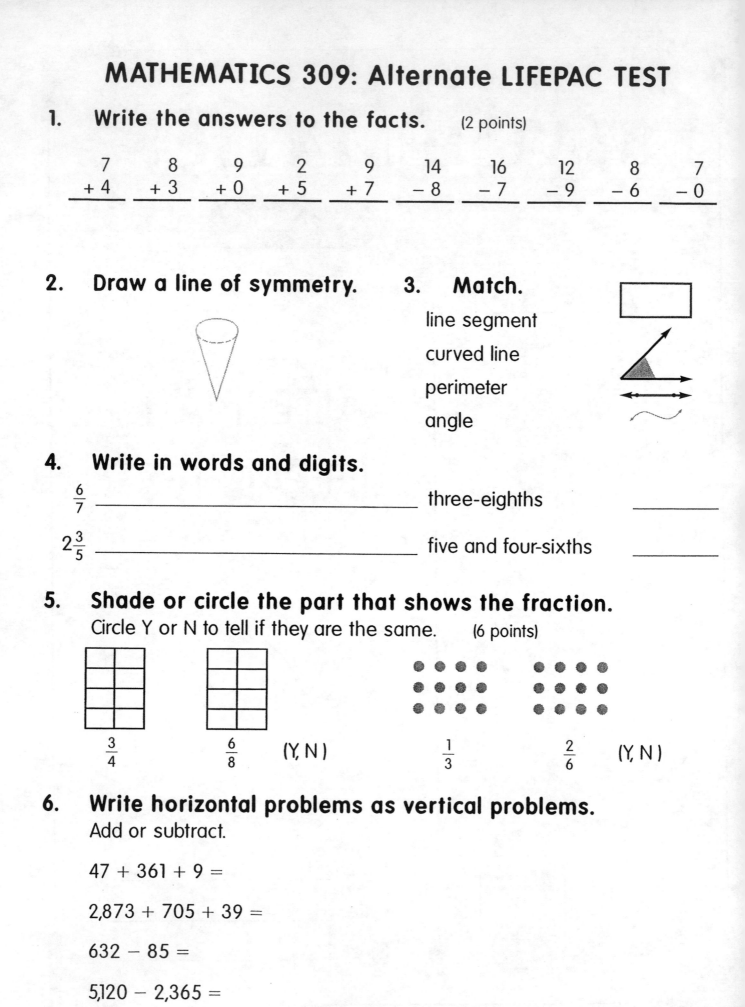

4. **Write in words and digits.**

$\frac{6}{7}$ _____   three-eighths   _____

$2\frac{3}{5}$ _____   five and four-sixths   _____

5. **Shade or circle the part that shows the fraction.**
   Circle Y or N to tell if they are the same. (6 points)

   $\frac{3}{4}$ $\frac{6}{8}$ (Y, N) $\frac{1}{3}$ $\frac{2}{6}$ (Y, N)

6. **Write horizontal problems as vertical problems.**
   Add or subtract.

   $47 + 361 + 9 =$

   $2{,}873 + 705 + 39 =$

   $632 - 85 =$

   $5{,}120 - 2{,}365 =$

7.   Circle the correct symbol.

5,746 (>, <) 5,764   8 + 7 − 9 (=, ≠) 15 + 2 − 9   70 − 30 (>, <) 60 − 40

8.   Write the correct temperatures.   0, 32, 100, 212

boiling = _____ degrees Fahrenheit   _____ degrees Celsius

9.   Write the name of the shape.

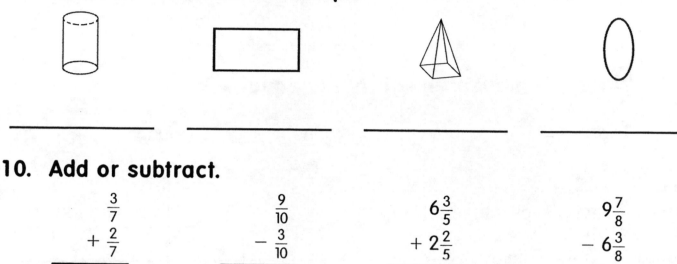

_____   _____   _____   _____

10. Add or subtract.

$$\frac{3}{7}$$
$$+ \frac{2}{7}$$
____

$$\frac{9}{10}$$
$$- \frac{3}{10}$$
____

$$6\frac{3}{5}$$
$$+ 2\frac{2}{5}$$
____

$$9\frac{7}{8}$$
$$- 6\frac{3}{8}$$
____

11.   Write the answers to the multiplication facts.   (5 points)

8 × 2 = _____   7 × 4 = _____   2 × 3 = _____   7 × 5 = _____

9 × 3 = _____   6 × 5 = _____   3 × 10 = _____   6 × 2 = _____

7 × 10 = _____   5 × 4 = _____

12. Find the area.

← 1 square yard

area _____

13. Write the number word.

3,052 _____

14. Round to thousands' place.

4,826 _____   7,500 _____   2,005 _____

15. Write in Roman numerals.   (2 points)

614 = _____ = _____ = _____

16. Write the measurement that is equal.

3 weeks = _____ days   2 tons = _____ pounds

17.

The line graph shows the number of students that ordered sodas for lunch at the cafeteria.
Write the number of students for each day.   (2 points)

Monday _____   Tuesday _____

Wednesday _____   Thursday _____

Friday _____

Soda Orders

MATHEMATICS

ALTERNATE
LIFEPAC TEST

40 / 50

Name_____

Date _____

Score _____

MATHEMATICS 310: Alternate LIFEPAC TEST

1. **Round the numbers.** Add or subtract both problems. (4 points)

$$
\begin{array}{ll}
315 \ \rule{2cm}{0.4pt} & 6{,}827 \ \rule{2cm}{0.4pt} \\
+\ 212 \ \rule{2cm}{0.4pt} & +\ 1{,}306 \ \rule{2cm}{0.4pt}
\end{array}
\qquad
\begin{array}{ll}
920 \ \rule{2cm}{0.4pt} & 6{,}946 \ \rule{2cm}{0.4pt} \\
-\ 580 \ \rule{2cm}{0.4pt} & -\ 2{,}180 \ \rule{2cm}{0.4pt}
\end{array}
$$

2. **Round the numbers.** Estimate the answer. (1 point)

Mrs. Gordon divided the books in the library by subject. There were 2,125 science books, 2,315 history books, and 4,536 story books. *About* how many books were there altogether?

_____ + _____ + _____ = _____

3. **Write the multiples for 3 and 4.** (4 points)

3 ___ ___ ___ ___ ___ ___ ___ ___ ___ ___

4 ___ ___ ___ ___ ___ ___ ___ ___ ___ ___

4. **Add or subtract.**

$$
\begin{array}{cccc}
\dfrac{2}{9} & \dfrac{3}{5} & \dfrac{9}{10} & \dfrac{7}{16} \\[6pt]
+\ \dfrac{4}{9} & +\ \dfrac{2}{5} & -\ \dfrac{3}{10} & -\ \dfrac{5}{16}
\end{array}
$$

$$
\begin{array}{cccc}
4\dfrac{1}{2} & 7\dfrac{3}{8} & 8\dfrac{5}{12} & 6\dfrac{2}{3} \\[6pt]
+\ 2\dfrac{1}{2} & +\ 2\dfrac{4}{8} & -\ 6\dfrac{1}{12} & -\ 5\dfrac{1}{3}
\end{array}
$$

5. **Write the answer.** Write the number of the rule.

    1) even and even or odd and odd = even

    2) odd and even or even and odd = odd

$$27 + 31 = \rule{1.5cm}{0.4pt}\ \rule{1.5cm}{0.4pt} \qquad\qquad 48 - 33 = \rule{1.5cm}{0.4pt}\ \rule{1.5cm}{0.4pt}$$

6. **Write the number of each kind of fish in the bowl.**
Write the probability for catching each kind of fish.   (4 points)

goldfish _____ or _____ out of _____.   tuna _____ or _____ out of _____.

dolphin _____ or _____ out of _____.   shark _____ or _____ out of _____.

7. **Add or subtract.** Check answers.   (4 points)

$$
\begin{array}{r} 428 \\ + 695 \\ \hline \end{array}
\qquad
\begin{array}{r} 2{,}367 \\ + 5{,}943 \\ \hline \end{array}
\qquad\qquad
\begin{array}{r} 600 \\ - 286 \\ \hline \\ + \\ \hline \end{array}
\qquad
\begin{array}{r} 7{,}054 \\ - 3{,}296 \\ \hline \\ + \\ \hline \end{array}
$$

8. **Write answers to the multiplication facts.**   (4 points)

$$
\begin{array}{r} 3 \\ \times 5 \\ \hline \end{array}
\quad
\begin{array}{r} 4 \\ \times 7 \\ \hline \end{array}
\quad
\begin{array}{r} 5 \\ \times 10 \\ \hline \end{array}
\quad
\begin{array}{r} 10 \\ \times 3 \\ \hline \end{array}
\quad
\begin{array}{r} 5 \\ \times 6 \\ \hline \end{array}
\quad
\begin{array}{r} 3 \\ \times 9 \\ \hline \end{array}
\quad
\begin{array}{r} 2 \\ \times 8 \\ \hline \end{array}
\quad
\begin{array}{r} 4 \\ \times 4 \\ \hline \end{array}
$$

9. **Find the perimeter and area.**

1 foot ⟶

perimeter _____

area _____

10. **Write the number word.**

456 _____

_____

3,054 _____

_____

11. **Write the measurer you would use.**

time to eat a hamburger _____

distance to your friend's house _____

12. Name the part of the drawing that is in gray.

_____   _____   _____   _____

13. Write in Roman numerals. (2 points)

$1{,}259$ = _____ = _____ = _____

14. Make the two sides of the problem equal.

$3 + 6 \neq 4 + 7$

_____

_____

15. Complete the two-step problem.

$18 + (7 - 2) =$ _____**?**_____

_____ = _____

16. Answer the questions. (1 point each lettered question)

a. If the minuend is 385 and the subtrahend is 279, what is the difference? _____

b. Corey's birthday is 5 days after John's. John's birthday is 9 days before David's. David's birthday is April 12. Give the date for each boy's birthday.

Corey _____ John _____ David _____

c. Megan has finished $\frac{5}{8}$ of her book.
How much of the book does she have left to read? _____

ANSWER KEYS

Part One

1.1

13	13	7	15	8	13	11	14	10
10	12	6	8	9	11	11	15	18
14	11	7	10	12	5	12	15	12
6	9	12	10	9	16	10	16	7
8	8	15	9	17	13	10	16	17
11	14	9	12	14	13	14	13	11

1.2

8	4	5	6	8	7	8	9	7
4	8	6	7	5	9	6	8	9
7	4	6	8	6	5	9	9	5
5	7	4	5	6	7	9	8	7
6	5	7	8	9	5	6	9	8
5	6	9	7	5	6	8	9	7

1.3

		2		5	6			9
10		12			16		18	
	21		23	25		27		
30			33	34			38	
		42		44		46		49
	51			55		57	58	
60		62		65				69
	71		73	74		76		
80				85		87		89
	91	92		94		96		
101	102	103	104	105	106	107	108	109

1.4   101

1.5   Teacher check

1.6

36	42	54	63	76	89	96
12	15	39	50	51	68	86

1.7
52, 54	39, 41	66, 68
17, 19	98, 100	30, 32
88, 90	44, 46	0, 2
21, 23	11, 13	105, 107

1.8   35, 37, 38, 40
99, 100, 102, 103

1.9
seven	fifty-eight
thirty	seventy-two
sixty-four	ninety-three
forty-one	nineteen
eighty-two	thirty-six

Part Two

2.1   3, 5

2.2
9, 8	7, 6
5, 4	3, 2
1, 7	5, 0
0, 9	2, 3

2.3
③0	3	①0	1
4	④0	7	⑦0
⑨0	9	⑧0	8

2.4
6, 2	9, 0
60, 2	90, 0
1, 1	0, 6
10, 1	0, 6

2.5   94, ninety-four
60, sixty
37, thirty-seven
20, twenty

2.6   6
7

2.7
95, 59	81, 18
43, 34	70, 7

2.8

18	36	76	68	99
58	74	48	17	88
89	47	57	89	68
85	99	58	79	85

2.9
	addend		addend
	addend		addend
77	sum	78	sum

2.10

26	12	33	10	45
44	68	26	75	94
56	79	60	63	42
36	18	62	43	21

2.11
	minuend		minuend
	subtrahend		subtrahend
55	difference	22	difference

2.12   8

2.13   8

2.14
4	5
15	19
20	20
14	9

2.15

+			
	6	9	11
	4	7	9
	10	13	15

+			
	11	9	4
	17	15	10
	13	11	6

Suggested Answers for 2.16 - 2.21:

2.16 73, 46, 92, 5, 84, 23, 53, 67, 49, 31

2.17 5, 23, 31, 46, 49, 53, 67, 73, 84, 92

2.18 5, 92
same

2.19 5, 32, 13, 64, 94, 35, 76, 37, 48, 29

2.20 5, 13, 29, 32, 35, 37, 48, 64, 76, 94

2.21 5, 94
less than 50

Part Three

3.1 200, 400, 500, 700, 900

3.2 361, 363   203, 205
794, 796   997, 999
800, 802   102, 104
648, 650   442, 444
499, 501   728, 730

3.3 420, 421, 422, 423, 424, 425, 426, 427,
428, 429

3.4 705, 715, 725, 735, 745, 755, 765, 775,
785, 795

3.5 64, 164, 264, 364, 464, 564, 664, 764,
864, 964

3.6 5, 4, 7

3.7 3, 7, 6
5, 4, 0

3.8 8, 6, 3   3, 4, 9
800, 60, 3   300, 40, 9

2, 2, 7   5, 6, 0
200, 20, 7   500, 60, 0

3.9 three hundred fifty-seven
four hundred two

3.10   addend   addend
addend   addend
969   sum   addend
15   sum

3.11 687   849   668   757
995   575   859   487
9   16   17   16   16   9
16   13   12   15   11   17

3.12   minuend
subtrahend
343   difference

3.13 772   123   452   580
375   462   164   446
415   325   342   263
460   543   772   543

3.14 12   36   3

3.15 Suggested Answers
ruler, 6 inches
ruler, 9 inches
ruler or yardstick, 36 inches or 1 yard
yardstick, 3 yards
yardstick, 16 yards

3.16 12
24
36
48

3.17 365 - three hundred sixty-five
70 - seventy
273 - two hundred seventy-three
653 - six hundred fifty-three
84 - eighty-four
112 - one hundred twelve
327 - three hundred twenty-seven
121 - one hundred twenty-one
48 - forty-eight
17 - seventeen

3.18 five hundred sixty
nine hundred thirteen
seven hundred four

Part Four

4.1 $8 + 7 = 15$

$6 - 2 \neq 5$

$15 > 14$

$27 < 30$

4.2 $\neq$ $-$

$<$ $-$

$=$ $+$

$>$ $+$

4.3   Suggested Answers:

8	5
7	20
11	2, 4
7	15, 8

4.4

$$59 \qquad \begin{array}{r} 17 \\ + 42 \\ \hline 59 \end{array}$$

$$32 \qquad \begin{array}{r} 53 \\ - 21 \\ \hline 32 \end{array}$$

$$22 \qquad \begin{array}{r} 63 \\ - 41 \\ \hline 22 \end{array}$$

$$675 \qquad \begin{array}{r} 987 \\ - 312 \\ \hline 675 \end{array}$$

$$254 \qquad \begin{array}{r} 895 \\ - 641 \\ \hline 254 \end{array}$$

$$557 \qquad \begin{array}{r} 533 \\ + 24 \\ \hline 557 \end{array}$$

$$696 \qquad \begin{array}{r} 256 \\ + 440 \\ \hline 696 \end{array}$$

$$740 \qquad \begin{array}{r} 780 \\ - 40 \\ \hline 740 \end{array}$$

4.5

43	38	52	70	95
31	21	53	74	30
75	51	81	70	92
63	95	73	66	72

4.6   fourth
second
seventh
first
eighth
ninth
sixth
third
fifth
tenth

4.7   9, 5, 3, 6, 11, 4, 7, 8
7, 3, 1, 10, 5, 6, 2, 4

4.8   6:48

4.9   3:53

4.10   8:15   1:35   10:22

4.11   24
60
60

4.12   February, June, November
12
Teacher check, 28, 31, 30
30, 31
Teacher check
Tuesday, Wednesday, Friday

4.13   7   30, 31   12
365 (366 - leap year)

4.14   Teacher check

Part Five

5.1   4   3   16   4   9   4   14   7

5.2   0, 1, 2, 3, 4, 5, 6, 7, 8, 9

5.3   58
23
607
three hundred fifty-five

5.4   2, 7, 9
      2, 70, 900

5.5   158, 159, 160, 161, 162

5.6   94, 93, 92, 91, 90

5.7   3 candles

5.8   12 > 10 or 10 < 12

5.9   7   14
      15   0

5.10 142 pennies
      22 pennies
      120 pennies
      142 pennies

5.11 12   36   3

5.12 inches   feet
      inch   yard
      feet   inches

5.13 12 apples
      5 apples
      2 apples

5.14 4
      50
      1
      2
      Teacher check
      3
      1
      3
      7
      12
      12
      5
      2
      12
      3
      12
      36
      2

5.15 358 - three hundred fifty-eight
      853 - eight hundred fifty-three
      538 - five hundred thirty-eight
      835 - eight hundred thirty-five
      385 - three hundred eighty-five
      583 - five hundred eighty-three

5.16 SUBTRAHEND

5.17   addend   minuend
          addend   subtrahend
      979 sum   632 difference

5.18 4:35
      Teacher check

5.19 1.   36   2.   46   3.   57
          + 4   + 23   + 27
          ----   ----   ----
            40   69   84

      4.   456   5.   243   6.   562
          + 42   + 616   + 213
          ----   -----   -----
           498   859   775

      7.   76   8.   49   9.   79
          + 58   + 83   − 3
          ----   ----   ----
           134   132   76

      10.   98   11.   18   12.   96
          − 51   − 5   − 64
          ----   ----   ----
            47   13   32

      13. 358   14. 498   15.   757
          − 34   − 252   − 340
          ----   -----   -----
           324   246   417

Part One

1.1 $4 + 6 = 10$, $10 - 4 = 6$, $10 - 6 = 4$
$14 - 6 = 8$, $6 + 8 = 14$, $8 + 6 = 14$
$5 + 8 = 13$, $13 - 5 = 8$, $13 - 8 = 5$
$9 - 8 = 1$, $1 + 8 = 9$, $8 + 1 = 9$
$9 + 7 = 16$, $16 - 7 = 9$, $16 - 9 = 7$

1.2 423, 523, 623, 723, 823, 923

1.3

+									
	5	11	9	6	12	8	7	6	3
	8	14	12	9	15	11	10	9	6

1.4 4, 5, 6, 7, 8, 9

1.5 $6 + 5 = 11$, $11 - 5 = 6$, $11 - 6 = 5$

1.6 138, 139, 140, 141, 142

1.7 81, 80, 79
minus one

1.8 8 worms
2, 4, 6, 8, ...

1.9

28	19	37	19	48
87	89	63	87	77
95	67	88	58	75
398	485	189	478	
685	799	758	689	
883	866	466	885	

1.10

6	8	8	13	16	11

1.11

30	55	71	64	50
64	84	48	80	82
90	83	57	66	91
74	82	52	90	31

1.12

55	72	47	13	86
80	44	75	17	50
33	82	46	19	72
256	517	623	982	
536	860	342	446	
252	217	417	379	

Part Two

2.1 tens   hundreds
ones   tens
hundreds   ones

2.2 8, 6, 3   4, 7, 9
800, 60, 3   400, 70, 9

5, 7, 0   2, 5, 8
500, 70, 0   200, 50, 8

2.3 0, 0, 0   place holder

2.4 578, 587, 758, 785, 857, 875

2.5 37, 73, 307, 370, 703, 730
37, 73

2.6 360, ones
407, tens
57
511
904, tens

2.7 307, 372, 426, 586, 587, 591

2.8

791	936	663	692	940

2.9

755	729	953	508	819

2.10

943	623	960	724
743	952	850	922

2.11

32	79	350	486
+ 55	+ 64	+ 73	+ 238
87	143	423	724

2.12 green circle - 10, 20, 30
blue line - 5, 10, 15, 20, 25, 30
red X - 2, 4, 6, 8, 10, 12, 14, 16, 18,
20, 22, 24, 26, 28, 30
0
0, 5
0, 2, 4, 6, 8

2.13

17	3
10	38
8	69
11	55

2.14 seventy-eight
three hundred eighty-two
four hundred nine
thirteen

2.15

33	944
11	306
50	512

2.16 70 - seventy
410 - four hundred ten
60 - sixty
287 - two hundred eighty-seven
119 - one hundred nineteen
563 - five hundred sixty-three
17 - seventeen

Part Three

3.1

8, 10	30, 32
138, 140	782, 784

3.2

7, 9	51, 53
263, 265	869, 871

3.3 Suggested Answer:
8, 10, 12, 14, 16

3.4 Suggested Answer:
5, 7, 9, 11, 13

3.5

94	112	634	834	720
95	92	780	832	825

3.6

$\frac{2}{3}$ $\frac{2}{5}$

$\frac{2}{4}$ $\frac{2}{6}$

3.7 one, two, three, four, five, six

3.8 first, second, third, fourth, fifth, sixth

3.9 two-thirds, two-fourths, two-fifths, two-sixths

3.10

$\frac{2}{3}$	$\frac{2}{4}$	$\frac{1}{3}$
two-thirds	two-fourths	one-third
$\frac{1}{2}$	$\frac{4}{6}$	$\frac{4}{5}$
one-half	four-sixths	four-fifths

$\frac{2}{6}$	$\frac{6}{10}$	$\frac{3}{4}$
two-sixths	six-tenths	three-fourths
$\frac{5}{8}$	$\frac{5}{6}$	$\frac{3}{7}$
five-eighths	five-sixths	three-sevenths

3.11

36	5	38	19	19
48	33	28	59	29
27	39	74	37	26
58	19	8	25	38

3.12

35, 37	962, 964
122, 124	508, 510
478, 480	717, 719
199, 201	300, 302

3.13 86, 406, 480, 486, 604, 840

3.14 950, 935, 905, 593, 530, 395

3.15

<	>	<
≠	=	≠
<	<	>
≠	=	=

3.16

thirteen	one hundred fifty-six
twenty-eight	three hundred nine
fifty-six	two hundred fifteen
forty	nine hundred eleven
seventy	eight hundred forty

3.17
634
748
571
260
419
353
25
96
487
999
121
99

Part Four

4.1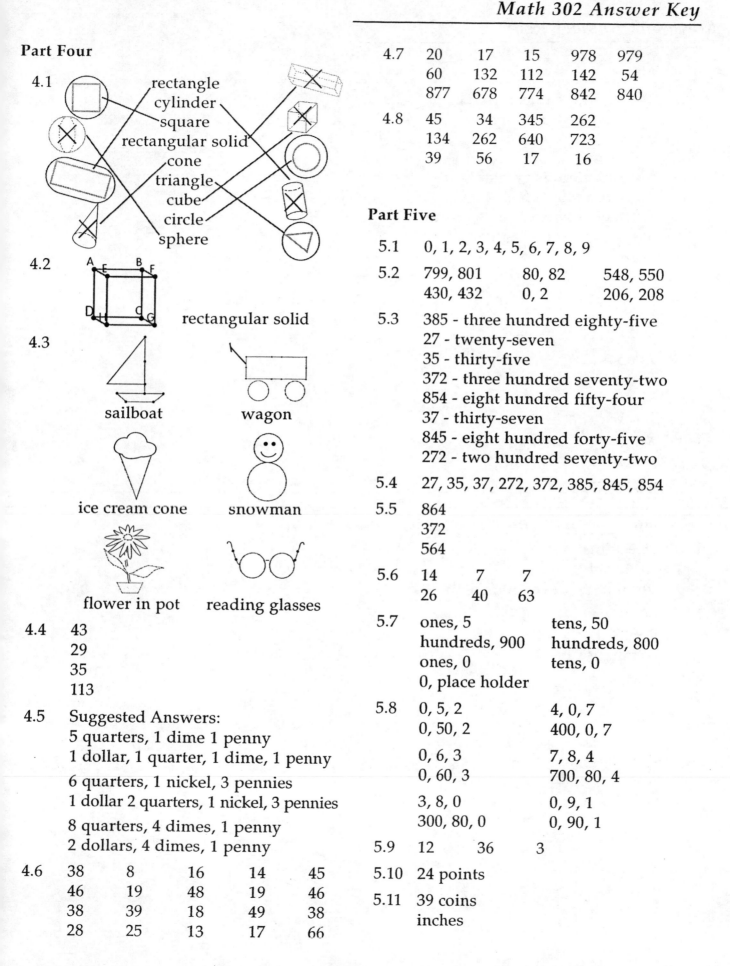

rectangle
cylinder
square
rectangular solid
cone
triangle
cube
circle
sphere

4.2

rectangular solid

4.3

sailboat   wagon

ice cream cone   snowman

flower in pot   reading glasses

4.4   43
29
35
113

4.5   Suggested Answers:
5 quarters, 1 dime 1 penny
1 dollar, 1 quarter, 1 dime, 1 penny

6 quarters, 1 nickel, 3 pennies
1 dollar 2 quarters, 1 nickel, 3 pennies

8 quarters, 4 dimes, 1 penny
2 dollars, 4 dimes, 1 penny

4.6

38	8	16	14	45
46	19	48	19	46
38	39	18	49	38
28	25	13	17	66

4.7

20	17	15	978	979
60	132	112	142	54
877	678	774	842	840

4.8

45	34	345	262
134	262	640	723
39	56	17	16

Part Five

5.1   0, 1, 2, 3, 4, 5, 6, 7, 8, 9

5.2

799, 801	80, 82	548, 550
430, 432	0, 2	206, 208

5.3   385 - three hundred eighty-five
27 - twenty-seven
35 - thirty-five
372 - three hundred seventy-two
854 - eight hundred fifty-four
37 - thirty-seven
845 - eight hundred forty-five
272 - two hundred seventy-two

5.4   27, 35, 37, 272, 372, 385, 845, 854

5.5   864
372
564

5.6

14	7	7
26	40	63

5.7

ones, 5	tens, 50
hundreds, 900	hundreds, 800
ones, 0	tens, 0
0, place holder	

5.8

0, 5, 2	4, 0, 7
0, 50, 2	400, 0, 7
0, 6, 3	7, 8, 4
0, 60, 3	700, 80, 4
3, 8, 0	0, 9, 1
300, 80, 0	0, 90, 1

5.9   12   36   3

5.10   24 points

5.11   39 coins
inches

5.12   8 feet

5.13   Twenty-three plus forty-six
       equals sixty-nine.
   Sixty-four plus thirty-seven
       is not equal to ninety-one.
   Six plus eight is greater than
       nine plus three.
   Thirteen minus seven is less than
       eighteen minus nine.

9	6	5
8	4	9
6	7	8
9	7	7
5	8	5
7	9	6
6	7	7
8	6	9
4	5	8
5	4	6

5.14
$$385 \qquad\qquad 83$$
$$\underline{+\ 456} \qquad\quad \underline{-\ 36}$$
$$841 \qquad\qquad 47$$

5.15   2:02   10:25   8:48   7:10

5.16   35 days
Thursday
31 days
Teacher check

5.17
Abby	Ken
Bruce	Laura
Cathy	Nora
Don	Tom
Jan	Will

5.18   three dots
10, 12, 14
count by 2's, even numbers

5.19
◎
R, S, T, U
rectangle

5.20 $1.90
$1.87
Lisa
3¢

5.21
18	7	13
15	11	17
11	14	9
11	7	15
9	16	8
8	10	8
6	16	11
12	9	13
10	10	14
12	12	13

Part One

1.1 $5 + 6 = 11$, $6 + 5 = 11$,
     $11 - 5 = 6$, $11 - 6 = 5$
     $3 + 4 = 7$, $4 + 3 = 7$,
     $7 - 3 = 4$, $7 - 4 = 3$
     $8 + 9 = 17$, $9 + 8 = 17$,
     $17 - 8 = 9$, $17 - 9 = 8$
     $6 + 7 = 13$, $7 + 6 = 13$,
     $13 - 6 = 7$, $13 - 7 = 6$

1.2 | | |
     |---|---|
     | 11 | 5 |
     | 6 | 16 |
     | 6 | 8 |
     | 0 | 6 |

1.3 12, 8, 13, 14, 9, 15, 11, 6
     3, 7, 5, 12, 4, 8, 6, 9

1.4 addend
     addend
     sum

1.5 | | | | | |
     |---|---|---|---|---|
     | 56 | 79 | 87 | 68 | 107 |
     | 33 | 94 | 134 | 100 | 102 |
     | 19 | 17 | 278 | 876 | 797 |
     | 362 | 816 | 725 | 851 | 522 |

1.6 6
     8, 4

1.7 | | | | | |
     |---|---|---|---|---|
     | 129 | 118 | 108 | 139 | 128 |
     | 131 | 103 | 171 | 170 | 149 |
     | 155 | 142 | 152 | 167 | 138 |

1.8 | | | | |
     |---|---|---|---|
     | 47 | 523 | 423 | 35 |
     | + 35 | + 184 | + 659 | 66 |
     | | | | + 21 |

1.9 | | | | | |
     |---|---|---|---|---|
     | 73 | 135 | 125 | 93 | 164 |
     | 128 | 121 | 128 | 165 | 180 |
     | 597 | 586 | 874 | 622 | 833 |
     | 739 | 870 | 773 | 712 | 504 |

1.10 603
      459
      352
      71
      126
      38

1.11 | | | |
      |---|---|---|
      | 50¢-bl | $1.00-gr | $1.50-or |
      | $1.00-gr | 50¢-bl | $1.00-gr |
      | 50¢-bl | $1.50-or | $1.50-or |

Part Two

2.1 Teacher check
cracker	book
eraser	carton of juice
ten pennies	bag of flour
box of cereal	friend
?	

2.2 | | | |
     |---|---|---|
     | P | O | P |
     | T | O | T |
     | O | O | O |
     | O/P | T | P |

2.3 16
     2
     2
     4

2.4 paper bag
     box of cereal
     toy box
     gallon of milk
     soup can
     salt shaker
     pop can

2.5 $3 + 8 = 11$, $8 + 3 = 11$,
     $11 - 3 = 8$, $11 - 8 = 3$
     $4 + 9 = 13$, $9 + 4 = 13$,
     $13 - 4 = 9$, $13 - 9 = 4$

2.6 $3 + 4 = 7$, $4 + 3 = 7$,
     $7 - 3 = 4$, $7 - 4 = 3$
     $7 + 9 = 16$, $9 + 7 = 16$,
     $16 - 7 = 9$, $16 - 9 = 7$
     $5 + 5 = 10$, $5 + 5 = 10$,
     $10 - 5 = 5$, $10 - 5 = 5$
     $7 + 0 = 7$, $0 + 7 = 7$,
     $7 - 0 = 7$, $7 - 7 = 0$
     $6 + 6 = 12$, $6 + 6 = 12$,
     $12 - 6 = 6$, $12 - 6 = 6$

2.7   83
      670

2.8   forty-nine   three hundred eighty-six
      seventy-six   seven hundred eight
      twelve   four hundred
      ninety   six hundred fifty

2.9   793, 739, 973, 937, 379, 397

2.10 379, 397, 739, 793, 937, 973

2.11 hundreds', ones'
      hundreds', ones'

2.12 126, 621   479, 974
      358, 853   58, 850
      234, 432   169, 961

2.13

109	115	81	102	78
18	14	112	109	132
567	896	859	752	

2.14

91	90	110	93	95
18	13	109	135	153
376	822	789	920	
513	566	849	980	
615	622	820	543	

Part Three

3.1   minuend
      subtrahend
      difference

3.2

17	23	49	37	24
8	37	29	42	28
236	508	824	238	

3.3

581	651	282	140
272	81	464	462
291	192	491	280
382	196	164	182

3.4 $73 > 68$

      $3 + 2 = 5$

      $\$2.25 < \$2.48$

      $3 + 4 \neq 4 + 2$

      $15 < 20$

      $12 - 5 = 7$

3.5   Six plus three is greater than
         twelve minus four.
      Eighteen minus nine is equal to
         two plus seven.
      Ninety-nine minus ten is not equal
         to eighty-eight plus ten.
      One hundred five is less than one
         hundred eleven.

3.6   6, 12, 14, 18
      9, 15, 21, 24
      10, 25, 35, 45
      30, 50, 60, 80

3.7

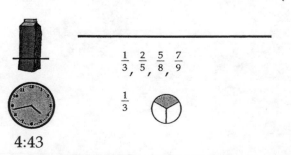

    10's   3's

    2's   5's

3.8

24	44	49	14
614	514	259	138
264	242	584	285

3.9   eleven
      forty-seven
      five hundred thirty-two
      four hundred six

      $8 + 3 = 9 + 2$
      $146 > 142$
      $8 \neq 13 - 4$
      $2 + 3 < 10 - 4$

      73, 72, 71, 70, 69, 68, 67, 66, 65, 64, 63

$\frac{1}{3}, \frac{2}{5}, \frac{5}{8}, \frac{7}{9}$

$\frac{1}{3}$

4:43

Part Four

4.1　4

$\frac{1}{4}$

one-fourth

yes

$\frac{1}{4}$

$\frac{2}{4}$

$\frac{3}{4}$

$\frac{4}{4}$

yes

4.2　8

$\frac{1}{8}$

one-eighth

yes

$\frac{1}{8}$

$\frac{2}{8}$

$\frac{3}{8}$

$\frac{4}{8}$

$\frac{8}{8}$

yes

4.3

45	88	84	96	60
90	99	158	133	138
22	17	13	14	14
134	149	146	190	131
77	83	94	96	82
575	684	588	795	
918	507	979	969	
984	758	856	957	
711	952	802	997	
980	639	880	703	

4.4　Suggested Answers
3 nickels, 2 pennies
1 quarter, 3 nickels, 1 penny
3 dimes, 2 pennies
2 quarters, 1 dime, 2 pennies

4.5　2
We are sleeping.
Teacher check
Suggested Answers:
　6:30 AM, 5:30 PM
Friday
Thursday, Saturday
Suggested Answers:
　7:00 AM
　8:00 AM
　9:30 AM
　2:30 PM
　3:15 PM
　9:00 PM

4.6
ones, 5	hundreds, 200
tens, 0	tens, 70
hundreds, 600	ones, 4
tens', 0, place holder	

4.7　400, 80, 5
600, 30, 0
50, 7

4.8　0, 1, 2, 3, 4, 5, 6, 7, 8, 9

4.9
7	125	40	524
284	4	83	8
65	86	376	304

Part Five

5.1

$\begin{array}{r}71\\23\\+48\\\hline \circled{81}\end{array}$ $\begin{array}{r}651\\326\\+325\\\hline \circled{751}\end{array}$ $\begin{array}{r}830\\571\\+259\\\hline \circled{831}\end{array}$ $\begin{array}{r}741\\318\\+423\\\hline 741\end{array}$

$\begin{array}{r}960\\851\\+109\\\hline \circled{950}\end{array}$ $\begin{array}{r}564\\310\\+254\\\hline 564\end{array}$ $\begin{array}{r}716\\327\\+389\\\hline 716\end{array}$ $\begin{array}{r}703\\412\\+291\\\hline \circled{603}\end{array}$

5.2
48	293	863	792
594	691	97	857

5.3 $3 + 6 = 9, 6 + 3 = 9,$
$9 - 3 = 6, 9 - 6 = 3$

$4 + 4 = 8, 4 + 4 = 8,$
$8 - 4 = 4, 8 - 4 = 4$

$0 + 5 = 5, 5 + 0 = 5,$
$5 - 0 = 5, 5 - 5 = 0$

5.4 4 months, 122 days
Tuesday, Thursday
48

5.5 40¢ 45¢ 55¢
Mark, Ben
Count money

5.6 $ .54 $ .60 $1.92
$3.07 $ .05 $ .42

5.7 $5.15 $4.02
$13.70 $6.03

5.8

square   triangle

rectangle

5.9

$\frac{7}{8}, \frac{1}{8}$

$\frac{8}{8}$

5.10 $146 + 122 = 268$
$146 > 122$

$5 + 3 + 2 = 10$
$10 < 18$

$7 - 5 = 2$
$5 < 7$

5.11

5.12 12   36   3
60   24
7   30, 31   365

5.13 11   53   1   12   21
16   26   17   25   49
115   285   608   493
153   116   44   267
383   423   81   62

Part One

1.1   0, 1, 2, 3, 4, 5, 6, 7, 8, 9

1.2   place holder

1.3   thousands   tens
     hundreds   ones
     ones   hundreds
     tens   thousands

1.4   1, 10, 100, 1,000
     8, 48, 270, 1,320

1.5   9,631
     4,280
     9,064

1.6

1,007	1,008	1,009	1,010	1,011
1,623	1,624	1,625	1,626	1,627
1,034	1,035	1,036	1,037	1,038

1.7

68	99	152	121	140
22	13	139	157	202
791	858	1,309	823	
1,103	985	1,209	891	
1,063	643	1,230	1,311	

1.8

1,095	998	1,186	1,179
985	1,099	789	1,298
1,388	1,099	1,044	1,357

1.9

14	20
18	22
11	11
8	19

1.10 tens, 50   ones, 5
     ones, 7   hundreds, 700
     tens, 0   hundreds, 200

1.11 20, 40, 50, 70, 90, 100
     10, 15, 25, 30, 35, 45
     6, 8, 10, 14, 16, 20
     0
     0, 5
     0, 2, 4, 6, 8

1.12

E	E	O	O
E	O	E	O

Part Two

2.1

60	10	90
100	60	70
50	60	20

2.2

80	90	20
30	30	40
50	40	70

2.3

20	90
10	30

2.4

       40   30
     + 60   + 40
   99   100   72   70

       70   50
     + 20   + 40
   90   90   93   90

       80   30
     + 20   + 40
  104   100   67   70

       60   30
     + 30   + 30
   91   90   57   60

2.5

9	21	49	28	39
119	416	526	604	148

2.6

164	263	575	592	272
494	284	383	53	281

2.7

289	227	167	478
169	372	285	146
599	179	174	388
288	276	289	72

2.8   length, time, volume, weight

2.9

12	36	3

2.10

60	60	24
30/31	12	365

2.11

16	2,000

2.12

16	2
2	4

2.13

3	4	5	6

2.14 $2\frac{1}{2}$, 3, $3\frac{1}{2}$, 4, $4\frac{1}{2}$, 5, $5\frac{1}{2}$, 6

2.15 $1\frac{1}{4}$, $1\frac{1}{2}$, $1\frac{3}{4}$

$4\frac{1}{4}$, $4\frac{1}{2}$, $4\frac{3}{4}$

2.16 Suggested Answers:

V, W	W	T
V	W	L
V, W	L	L

Part Three

3.1 $3 + 4 = 7$, $4 + 3 = 7$,
$7 - 3 = 4$, $7 - 4 = 3$
$9 + 9 = 18$, $9 + 9 = 18$,
$18 - 9 = 9$, $18 - 9 = 9$
$2 + 6 = 8$, $6 + 2 = 8$,
$8 - 2 = 6$, $8 - 6 = 2$
$5 + 5 = 10$, $5 + 5 = 10$,
$10 - 5 = 5$, $10 - 5 = 5$
$9 + 3 = 12$, $3 + 9 = 12$,
$12 - 3 = 9$, $12 - 9 = 3$
$3 + 0 = 3$, $0 + 3 = 3$,
$3 - 0 = 3$, $3 - 3 = 0$
$7 + 9 = 16$, $9 + 7 = 16$,
$16 - 7 = 9$, $16 - 9 = 7$

3.2

+				
	17	15	10	16
	11	9	4	10
	8	6	1	7

3.3 12, 9, 6, 8, 10, 11, 7, 13

3.4 cups   inches   feet
yards   dozen   hour

3.5 one hundred forty-three
nine hundred five
four hundred seventy-six

3.6 four thousand, nine hundred thirty
two thousand, eight hundred fifteen
six thousand, four hundred
   seventy-two

3.7 eight thousand, forty-seven
nine thousand, sixty
two thousand, thirteen

two thousand, five
seven thousand, two

3.8 4   3   8   9

3.9

6	5	8	2
8	0	3	1
2	3	0	8

3.10 6,000, 600, 20, 0
100, 80, 5
3,000, 200, 10, 3
7,000, 400, 60, 0

3.11 6,085

3.12 hundreds, thousands, ones, tens

3.13

4,861, 4,863	3,050, 3,052
8,004, 8,006	1,998, 2,000
9,900, 9,902	4,368, 4370

3.14 7,733   8,648   4,340
9,299   6,999   8,100

3.15 3,284   3,824   4,382
          4,823   8,342   8,423

3.16 one-fourth
three-eighths
five-sixths

3.17 $\frac{5}{8}$ $\frac{6}{7}$ $\frac{1}{2}$

3.18 Suggested Answers:

3		8	1	1
2	6	3	1	1
5		3	1	3
5	1	1		3
12	3			1
12		7	1	1

3.19

9:30

$7 - 4 = 3$
April
$2\frac{1}{2}$ inches

$40 < 50$
12

3.20
>	>	<
<	>	>
<	<	<
≠	=	≠
=	=	≠
≠	≠	=

greater than
greater than
equal to
not equal to

3.21   3, 6, 8   5, 3,   2

3.22   3, 9   6, 5   8

3.23

205	45	863	315
351	63	4	27
+ 32	+ 251	+ 29	+ 542
588	359	896	884

849	791	673	725
− 236	− 254	− 68	− 36
613	537	605	689

Part Four

4.1   5, 1, 1, 7
      10, 1, 1, 1, 13
      10, 10, 1, 1, 22
      50, 10, 5, 65

4.2

4.3   3, 6, 9, 12, 15, 18, 21, 24, 27, 30

4.4   3, 6, 9, 12, 15, 18, 21, 24, 27, 30

4.5   lines
      curved, straight
      end points
      lines, end points

4.6   4   26   32   50   72   58
      0, 2, 4, 6, 8

4.7 $\frac{1}{4} + \frac{2}{4} = \frac{3}{4}$

      $\frac{4}{9} + \frac{3}{9} = \frac{7}{9}$

$\frac{2}{3} + \frac{1}{3} = \frac{3}{3}$

$\frac{2}{6} + \frac{2}{6} = \frac{4}{6}$

$\frac{3}{12} + \frac{4}{12} = \frac{7}{12}$

$\frac{3}{8} + \frac{3}{8} = \frac{6}{8}$

4.8 $\frac{3}{4} - \frac{1}{4} = \frac{2}{4}$

$\frac{6}{9} - \frac{2}{9} = \frac{4}{9}$

$\frac{3}{3} - \frac{2}{3} = \frac{1}{3}$

$\frac{5}{6} - \frac{1}{6} = \frac{4}{6}$

$\frac{9}{12} - \frac{4}{12} = \frac{5}{12}$

$\frac{5}{8} - \frac{2}{8} = \frac{3}{8}$

4.9
14	13	95	163	141
69	83	156	81	77
782	868	829	845	1,145
751	832	864	999	1,197

4.10
11	22	44	56	37
22	34	44	36	26
122	341	253	245	207
673	261	62	65	136

Part Five

5.1   9, 5
      9, 4

      $5 + 4 = 9, 9 - 4 = 5,$

      $4 + 5 = 9, 9 - 5 = 4$

5.2 264
603
2,435

5.3 131
781

5.4 1, 6, 5, 3, 7, 2, 4

5.5 0, 1, 2, 3, 4, 5, 6, 7, 8, 9
0, place holder

5.6 two-thirds   five-eighths
one-half   three-ninths

$\frac{4}{5}$ $\frac{2}{9}$

$\frac{7}{8}$ $\frac{6}{11}$

numerator

fraction bar

denominator

5.7 $\frac{2}{3}$ glass of milk
$\frac{4}{9}$ set of marbles
6, 18, 24, 4, 10, 16,
12, 2 (even)
8, 6
no

5.8 V   VIII   XIII
3, 2, 5   5, 3, 8   7, 6, 13
V   VI   VII
7, 2, 5   11, 5, 6   15, 8, 7

5.9 43¢ or $ .43   65¢ or $ .65
$5.22
$16.30

5.10 $5.50
30 crayons
60 stones
90 steps

5.11 thirty-three
eleven
one hundred five
seven hundred fifty
eight thousand, six hundred
forty-nine

5.12
24	436	94	325
36	28	− 8	− 47
+ 51	+ 5	86	278
111	469		

5.13 28
25
Ken

5.14 4   4   3   0

5.15 $12 > 7$
$2 + 4 = 6$
$4 + 20 \neq 13 + 10$

5.16 rectangular solid
cylinder
sphere
cube

5.17
28	199	504	2,759
52	59	248	3,679

968, 969, 970, 971, 972, 973

356	27	840	4,368
24	182	607	581
7	36	211	2,883

3286	2386	8326	
	6623	2836	8263
2386	2836	3286	
	6623	8263	8326

five thousand, two hundred
sixty-three
four thousand, eight hundred five

Part One

1.1	2,638	4,020	6,999	
1.2	99	361	519	1,432
	74	250	900	1,658

1.3

3,003	3,005
~~3,013~~	~~3,050~~
5,287	5,290
~~5,278~~	~~5,209~~
7,635	7,638
~~7,653~~	~~7,338~~

1.4	53	640	8,732
	62	953	9,641

1.5	4	52	476	1,588

1.6

tens	hundreds	ones
tens	thousands	hundreds
ones	hundreds	tens

1.7 Twenty-four plus sixty-three equals eighty-seven.
Seventy-five minus twenty-two equals fifty-three.
One hundred twenty-four plus two hundred thirty-five equals three hundred fifty-nine.
Nine hundred twenty-six minus four hundred fourteen equals five hundred twelve.

1.8

32	429	76	648
+ 63	+ 215	− 51	− 122
95	644	25	526

1.9

+, =	+, =	−, =
−, =	−, =	+(−), =

1.10

addend	minuend
addend	subtrahend
sum	difference

1.11

19	173	127	988	975
101	941	847	643	803
23	19	207	455	177
47	48	56	261	578

1.12

1st	second
2nd	fifth
3rd	fourth
4th	first
5th	third

6th	eighth
7th	tenth
8th	ninth
9th	sixth
10th	seventh

1.13

twenty-third	87
fifty-sixth	32
ninety-first	23
thirty-second	56
eighty-seventh	91

thirteen	45
sixtieth	18
seventy-fourth	13
forty-fifth	74
eighteenth	60

1.14	12	36	3	
1.15	4:05	8:55	3:58	7:11
1.16	13	12	16	9	7

1.17

	numerator
fraction bar	
	denominator

1.18

$\frac{4}{7}$	$\frac{5}{9}$	$\frac{1}{2}$
$\frac{3}{15}$	$\frac{7}{12}$	$\frac{2}{8}$

1.19

two-eighths	seven-ninths
three-fifths	six-eighths
four-sevenths	two-thirds

1.20

$\frac{3}{4}$	$\frac{4}{5}$	$\frac{5}{8}$
$\frac{9}{15}$	$\frac{7}{9}$	$\frac{3}{6}$

1.21

$\frac{3}{5}$	$\frac{7}{8}$	$\frac{9}{12}$	$\frac{2}{7}$	$\frac{1}{9}$	$\frac{2}{6}$

Part Two

2.1 7, 4, 6, 3
7,000, 400, 60, 3

8, 4, 0
800, 40, 0
5, 6
50, 6

9, 2, 0, 1
9,000, 200, 0, 1

2.2 Suggested Answers:

4,763 - 60
4,673 - 600
4,736 - 6
6,473 - 6,000
6,743 - 6,000
4,673 - 600

2.3 1,427   1,202   1,311   1,083   1,663
734   1,670   1,145   961   1,444

2.4 2, 4, 6, 8, 10, 12, 14, 16, 18, 20
5, 10, 15, 20, 25, 30, 35, 40, 45, 50
3, 6, 9, 12, 15, 18, 21, 24, 27, 30

2.5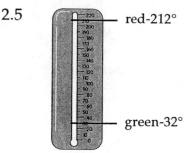
red-212°
green-32°

2.6 Suggested Answers:
ice skating
December, January
85 degrees F.
swimming
July, August

2.7 Suggested Answers:
74   32
48   70
98   120
up
ice water

Measured Temperatures

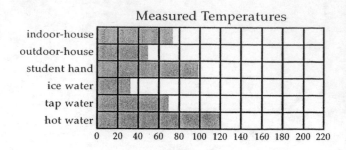

2.8 Thirty-seven plus forty-five is equal to eighty-two.
Eighty-nine minus thirty-four is not equal to fifty-seven.
Four plus nine is greater than five plus six.
Seventeen minus eight is less than eight plus eight.

2.9 $25 + 63 = 88$
$97 - 43 \neq 55$
$6 + 4 > 3 + 5$
$16 - 4 < 19 - 2$

2.10 $\neq$ $=$ $=$
$\neq$ $\neq$ $\neq$

2.11 $<$ $<$ $>$
$>$ $<$ $>$

2.12 189   167   675   477   354
179   169   378   675   267

2.13 $2 + 3 = 7, 17 - 8 = 6$
$5 + 9 = 13, 11 - 8 = 6$
$12 - 5 = 8, 16 - 5 = 8$
$3 - 3 = 3, 6 - 3 = 2$
$8 + 7 = 13, 8 - 0 = 0$

Part Three

3.1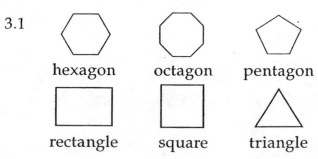

hexagon   octagon   pentagon

rectangle   square   triangle

3.2

400	400	900
100	800	600
600	500	1,000

3.3

500	400	900
300	600	500
200	600	900

3.4

20	60	40
40	90	80
70	30	90

3.5

$$\begin{array}{r} 300 \\ + 500 \\ \hline 779 \quad 800 \end{array} \qquad \begin{array}{r} 300 \\ + 300 \\ \hline 630 \quad 600 \end{array}$$

$$\begin{array}{r} 200 \\ + 400 \\ \hline 607 \quad 600 \end{array} \qquad \begin{array}{r} 500 \\ + 200 \\ \hline 687 \quad 700 \end{array}$$

$$\begin{array}{r} 500 \\ + 200 \\ \hline 688 \quad 700 \end{array} \qquad \begin{array}{r} 300 \\ + 500 \\ \hline 789 \quad 800 \end{array}$$

$$\begin{array}{r} 300 \\ + 300 \\ \hline 571 \quad 600 \end{array} \qquad \begin{array}{r} 800 \\ + 100 \\ \hline 945 \quad 900 \end{array}$$

3.6 Suggested Answers:

8	7	6

3.7 6, 4, 6, 4, 20
24

3.8 $3\frac{1}{2}$

$1\frac{1}{4}$

$2\frac{3}{4}$

3.9 $1\frac{1}{2}, 1\frac{1}{2}, 1\frac{1}{2}, 4\frac{1}{2}, 4\frac{1}{2}$

$2, 1\frac{1}{4}, 2, 1\frac{1}{4}, 6\frac{2}{4}(\frac{1}{2}), 6\frac{2}{4}(\frac{1}{2})$

1, 1, 1, 1, 1, 5, 5

3.10

131	115	139
879	1,143	1,032
18	38	27
216	181	547

3.11 6
20
0
15
9
11

Part Four

4.1 circle - 2, 4, 6, 8, 10, 12, 14, 16, 18
line - 1, 3, 5, 7, 9, 11, 13, 15, 17

4.2

14	16	9	5
E, E, E	O, O, E	E, O, O	O, E, O

4.3 even
odd

4.4

14	12
O, O, E - yes	E, E, E - yes
9	5
O, E, O - yes	E, O, O - yes
9	8
E, O, O - yes	O, O, E - yes

4.5 Lines of symmetry may vary.

hexagon   pentagon   triangle

rectangle   octagon   square

4.6 43 - forty-three
246 - two hundred forty-six
464 - four hundred sixty-four
3,464 - three thousand, four hundred sixty-four
6,434 - six thousand, four hundred thirty-four
2,460 - two thousand, four hundred sixty
4,640 - four thousand, six hundred forty
264 - two hundred sixty-four
3,644 - three thousand, six hundred forty-four
26 - twenty-six

4.7
26
43
246
264
464
2,460
3,464
3,644
4,640
6,434

4.8

139	121	599	1,113	663
12	20	117	155	1,210
607	1,183	1,534	1,083	1,053

4.9

33	51	21	24	27
612	370	414	117	214
356	287	346	37	159

4.10 $X + I + I = 10 + 1 + 1 = 12$

$V + I + I = 5 + 1 + 1 = 7$

$X + X + V = 10 + 10 + 5 = 25$

4.11 $X + V - I = 10 + 5 - 1 = 14$

$X + X + V - I = 10 + 10 + 5 - 1 = 24$

$X + X + X - I = 10 + 10 + 10 - 1 = 29$

4.12 $75 < 95$

$842 > 832$

$13 - 8 \neq 4 + 4$

$64 + 48 = 112$

4.13 $\frac{4}{5}$ $\frac{6}{8}$ $\frac{2}{2}$ $\frac{6}{7}$ $\frac{8}{12}$ $\frac{8}{9}$

$\frac{2}{4}$ $\frac{3}{7}$ $\frac{5}{8}$ $\frac{2}{5}$ $\frac{5}{12}$ $\frac{6}{15}$

4.14 three-fifths
one-half
six-eighths

4.15 $\frac{1}{8}$ $\frac{4}{7}$ $\frac{2}{9}$

4.16

+					
	5	10	9	2	8
	12	17	16	9	15
	8	13	12	5	11

−					
	8	5	10	6	9
	6	3	8	4	7
	3	0	5	1	4

Part Five

5.1 460
VIII
17

M
1
4,382

5.2

5.3

| 6 | 5 | 8 | 7 | 8 | 6 |
| 4 | 2 | 6 | 0 | 9 | 10 |

5.4

paint	bread
crayons	jack-in-the-box
toothbrush	book

5.5 30
80
70
50
300
900

5.6 40, 80

5.7

| 60 | 60 | 24 |
| 30/31 | 12 | 365 |

40 minutes
30 minutes
2 days or 2\7 week
October
350
45 seconds
22 hours

134

5.8   5,687   5,867   6,857
      7, 586   7, 856   8, 687

5.9   7,861   6,849   8,999   4,636
      9,552   4,000   5,687   2,361

5.10

How Much Do Pet Dogs Weigh

	0	10	20	30	40	50	60	70	80	90	100
Jim's dog											
Seans dog											
Mark's dog											
Corey's dog											
Jason's dog											

5.11 Three hundred twenty-five plus
      four hundred fifty-six equals
      seven hundred eighty-one.
      Eight hundred thirty-two minus
      five hundred nine equals three
      hundred twenty-three.
      Two hundred three is less than two
      hundred thirteen
      Six plus eight is greater than seven
      plus five.

5.12 8 books
      2:45 PM
      1 hour(It takes 15 minutes to walk
      home.)
      175 history books
      344 books
      Tuesday, March 28

5.13
$$\begin{array}{r}\frac{1}{4}\\+\frac{2}{4}\\\hline\frac{3}{4}\end{array}\qquad\begin{array}{r}\frac{7}{8}\\-\frac{3}{8}\\\hline\frac{4}{8}\end{array}\qquad\begin{array}{r}\frac{1}{5}\\+\frac{4}{5}\\\hline\frac{5}{5}\end{array}\qquad\begin{array}{r}\frac{8}{9}\\-\frac{5}{9}\\\hline\frac{3}{9}\end{array}$$

Part One

1.1   addend
      addend
      addend
      sum

1.2   17   112   155   133   569
      682   730   910   981   1,443

1.3   7,796   8,589   9,717   4,677

1.4   5,816   7,060   8,633   8,711
      9,223   9,314   5,799   3,120

1.5   3,859   5,995   2,405
      5,292   6,400   8,000

1.6   6,458   6,845   8,456
      8,564   8,645   8,654

1.7   2, 4, 6, 8, 10, 12, 14, 16, 18, 20
      3, 6, 9, 12, 15, 18, 21, 24, 27, 30
      5, 10, 15, 20, 25, 30, 35, 40, 45, 50
      10, 20, 30, 40, 50, 60, 70, 80, 90, 100

1.8   2, 3   2, 5, 10
      3, 5   3, 5, 10   note: Some students may
                        have circled 2. 2 is also a
                        correct answer. 30 is a
                        multiple of 2 (15 x 2 = 30)
                        but is not shown in ex. 1.7.

1.9   F R I E N D S

1.10 38   26   29   53
      E, E, E   O, O, E   E, O, O   O, E, O

      even
      odd

1.11 54   82
      O, O, E, yes   E, E, E, yes

      79   107
      O, E, O, yes   E, O, O, yes

1.12 36
      48
      24
      12

1.13 9:45 A.M.   1:12 P.M.   3:05   6:56

1.14 digital
      dial
      minute
      hour
      second
      A.M.
      P.M.

1.15 60   60   24
      30/31   12   365

      15

      6:15
      8:45

Part Two

2.1   minuend
      subtrahend
      difference

2.2   14   16   26   512   123
      572   323   272   137   286

2.3   2,122   5,902   2,622   5,021

2.4   Suggested Answers:
      6
      28
      47
      93
      62
      15
      4, 29
      57
      22
      2 (28, 4)

2.5   13   16   11   8   17   10

2.6   6   2   4   0   8   3

2.7   12   36   3

2.8   10 linear inches
      10 linear feet
      10 linear yards
      10 linear miles

2.9　20
　　　20
　　　24
　　　24

2.10　144

2.11　Suggested Answer:
　　　15 square feet

2.12　Suggested Answers:
　　　floor of room = 40 square feet
　　　floor mat = 12 square feet
　　　rug = 15 square feet
　　　desk = 9 square feet

2.13　　　　　　　　numerator
　　　fraction bar
　　　　　　　　denominator

2.14　$\frac{5}{5}$　　$\frac{7}{9}$　　$\frac{12}{16}$　　$\frac{3}{7}$　　$\frac{4}{8}$　　$\frac{5}{16}$

2.15
$$\begin{array}{r}\frac{3}{8}\\+\frac{4}{8}\\\hline\frac{7}{8}\end{array}\qquad\begin{array}{r}\frac{2}{9}\\+\frac{3}{9}\\\hline\frac{5}{9}\end{array}\qquad\begin{array}{r}\frac{6}{10}\\-\frac{2}{10}\\\hline\frac{4}{10}\end{array}\qquad\begin{array}{r}\frac{9}{15}\\-\frac{3}{15}\\\hline\frac{6}{15}\end{array}$$

2.16　5　　16
　　　12　　9

2.17　0, 2, 8, 3
　　　0, 200, 80, 3

　　　2, 9, 0, 4
　　　2,000, 900, 0, 4

　　　4, 0, 0, 6
　　　4,000, 0, 0, 6

　　　0, 0, 8, 4
　　　0, 0, 80, 4

2.18　Suggested Answers:　3,517 = 7
　　　　　　　　　　　　　3,571 = 70
　　　　　　　　　　　　　3,751 = 700
　　　　　　　　　　　　　7,351 = 7,000
　　　　　　　　　　　　　3,715 = 700
　　　　　　　　　　　　　3,157 = 7

2.19　478　8,740　　567　7,650
　　　136　6,310　　269　9,620
　　　0
　　　place holder

2.20　=　　<　　≠
　　　>　　=　　>

Part Three

3.1　17　　71　　765　　895　　1,773
　　　4,940　9,778　3,992　8,661　8,432
　　　6,804　8,887　7,503　8,892　8,897

3.2　3,057
　　　6,817
　　　2,629
　　　7,307
　　　5,109
　　　6,121

3.3　$\frac{1}{2}$　　$\frac{2}{4}$　　$\frac{4}{8}$
　　　$\frac{1}{2},\frac{2}{4},\frac{4}{8}$

3.4　$\frac{1}{3}$　　$\frac{2}{6}$　　$\frac{4}{12}$
　　　numerator
　　　$\frac{1}{3},\frac{2}{6},\frac{4}{12}$

3.5　$\frac{1}{2}$　　$\frac{2}{4}$　　$\frac{4}{8}$
　　　$\frac{1}{2},\frac{2}{4},\frac{4}{8}$

3.6　$\frac{1}{3}$　　$\frac{2}{6}$　　$\frac{4}{12}$
　　　numerator
　　　$\frac{1}{3},\frac{2}{6},\frac{4}{12}$

3.7
$$\begin{array}{r}57¢\\+35¢\\\hline92¢\end{array}$$

$$\begin{array}{r}\$5.60\\+\$6.28\\\hline\$11.88\end{array}$$

$$\begin{array}{r}\$1.29\\-\$.35\\\hline\$.94\end{array}$$

$$\begin{array}{r}\$5.45\\-\$1.28\\\hline\$4.17\end{array}$$

3.8 L + X, 50 + 10, 60

L + V + I + I, 50 + 5 + 1 + 1, 57

L + V − I, 50 + 5 − 1, 54

C + X + V − I, 100 + 10 + 5 − 1, 114

D + C − X, 500 + 100 − 10, 590

M + C + X + V,

1,000 + 100 + 10 + 5, 1,115

3.9 50   20   70   30   100   30

3.10 400   600   200   800   500   300

3.11 ~~50~~   ~~40~~   ~~300~~   ~~600~~

30   90   500   300

82 80   128 130   794 800   900 900

3.12 53   45   411   606   658

322   224   256   181   586

3,131   5,731   216   265   289

3.13 7, 6, 3, 9, 4, 5, 8, 12

12, 10, 15, 13, 8, 9, 11, 7

Part Four

4.1 2, 4, 6, 8, 10, 12, 14, 16, 18, 20

4.2 10   12

14   16

18   20

4.3 2   4   6   8

10   12   14   16

18   20

six, fourteen

4.4

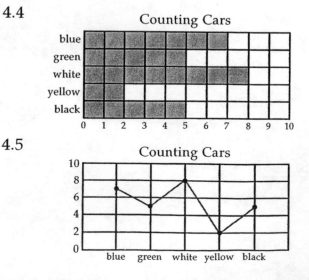

Counting Cars

4.5

Counting Cars

4.6

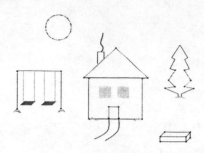

yes

4.7 4 + 7 = 11, 7 + 4 = 11,

11 − 4 = 7, 11 − 7 = 4

6 + 8 = 14, 8 + 6 = 14,

14 − 6 = 8, 14 − 8 = 6

3 + 5 = 8, 5 + 3 = 8,

8 − 3 = 5, 8 − 5 = 3

7 + 9 = 16, 9 + 7 = 16,

16 − 7 = 9, 16 − 9 = 7

4.8 30   80   35   105

4.9 <   ≠   −

>   =   +

4.10 2,067   2,654   2,670

3,456   3,645   5,465

4.11 2,793

4,852

6,073

5,481

4.12 3 + 5 = 2 + 6

30 − 0 = 28 + 2

41 < 56

15 − 8 ≠ 6

4 + 1 = 6 − 1

85 > 65

30 + 2 < 35

3 × 2 = 6

4.13 fifty-six

seven hundred five

three thousand, fifty-five

Six plus four is not equal to eleven.

Seventy-six is greater than

forty-nine.

4.14 2, 4, 6, 8, 10, 12, 14, 16, 18, 20

138

4.15	2	4	6	8
	10	12	14	16
		18	20	

4.16	115	130	212	1,042	1,065
	5,969	8,576	7,463	8,934	7,422

4.17	52	29	224	604	266
	617	569	448	368	334
	151	364	279	3,233	1,401

Part Five

5.1 Suggested Answers:

1	2	3	4	9	10	11	12
$+7$	$+6$	$+5$	$+4$	-1	-2	-3	-4
8	8	8	8	8	8	8	8

5.2 10, 20, 30, 40, 50, 60, 70, 80, 90, 100

5.3 646

5.4 $\frac{6}{9}$, six-ninths

5.5 $1.19

5.6 36 marbles

5.7 perimeter
area

5.8 yes, no

5.9 144   9

5.10 367 miles

5.11 5,280 linear feet

5.12 red

5.13

$$\frac{2}{7} + \frac{4}{7} = \frac{6}{7} \qquad \frac{3}{5} + \frac{1}{5} = \frac{4}{5} \qquad \frac{5}{10} + \frac{3}{10} = \frac{8}{10}$$

5.14

$$\frac{5}{8} - \frac{4}{8} = \frac{1}{8} \qquad \frac{7}{9} - \frac{5}{9} = \frac{2}{9} \qquad \frac{4}{6} - \frac{3}{6} = \frac{1}{6}$$

5.15

octagon
triangle
square
hexagon
rectangle
pentagon

5.16 Chapter 18

5.17 703

5.18 0, 2, 4, 6, 8
1, 3, 5, 7, 9

162, 8, 426, 700, 354
37, 1,263, 9,999, 5,441, 805

5.19 ones   tens
hundreds   ones
hundreds   thousands

5.20 $\frac{1}{6}$

5.21 eight thousand, four hundred six
five thousand, forty-nine

5.22	60	60	24
	30/31	12	365

5.23 year, month, date, day

12	6	8	2
9	3	5	1
11	7	4	10

Tuesday, May 15

5.24 odd
Wednesday
May 22
Thursday
May 25
4 + 11 + 18 + 25 = 58
2 + 8 − 5 + 11 = 16
2, 4, 6, 8, 10, 12, 14, 16, 18, 20
Thursday, Wednesday
Friday
May 24

Math 307 Answer Key

Part One

1.1   0, 1, 2, 3, 4, 5, 6, 7, 8, 9

1.2   Suggested Answers:
3, 7
46, 78
205, 582
5,368, 7,428
382, 1,083

1.3   Suggested Answers:

29	95
936	9,347
9,347	29

1.4   182   1,491   1,024   7,498   8,858

1.5   6,274   7,345   8,592   8,977
3,610   7,799   9,521   8,404

1.6   39   627   353   275   2,223

1.7   1,488   3,754   5,509   1,687
2,778   2,887   1,789   1,868

1.8   2, 4, 6, 8, 10, 12, 14, 16, 18, 20
3, 6, 9, 12, 15, 18, 21, 24, 27, 30
5, 10, 15, 20, 25, 30, 35, 40, 45, 50
10, 20, 30, 40, 50, 60, 70, 80, 90, 100

1.9

2	4	6	8
10	12	14	16
	18	20	

1.10

5	10	15	20
25	30	35	40
	45	50	

1.11

times	times
six	eight
times	times
fifteen	twenty

1.12

F	M	M	W
M	W	F	M

1.13   two-thirds   five-eighths
four-ninths   three-sixths

1.14   three and two-fifths
four and five-eighths
six and one-seventh
five and two-thirds

Part Two

2.1

16	2,000
16	2
2	4

2.2

12	36
5,280	3
144	9

2.3   18 linear feet
18 square feet

22 linear yards
28 square yards

2.4   14 linear inches
7 square inches

16 linear feet
7 square feet

2.5   Suggested Answers:

P	O	T	T
P	O	O	P
O/P	P/Q/G	O	G
O	O	O	O/Q
H			
Y			
M			
Mh			

2.6   169   327   139   619   68
227   273   268   116   118

2.7

18	19
12	14

2.8   400   40   4,000

2.9 $\frac{6}{7}$ $\frac{5}{8}$ $\frac{2}{2}$ $\frac{1}{5}$ $\frac{3}{9}$ $\frac{5}{12}$

2.10 $3\frac{4}{5}$ $7\frac{4}{7}$ $9\frac{4}{8}$ $6\frac{5}{6}$
$5\frac{2}{8}$ $4\frac{2}{7}$ $4\frac{4}{12}$ $3\frac{1}{5}$

2.11   Two and three-fifths plus one and one-fifth is equal to three and four-fifths.

2.12   Seven and five-eighths minus two and three-eighths is equal to five and two-eighths.

2.13 4   6   5   7
    E, E, E   O, O, E   O, E, O   E, O, O
    even
    odd

2.14 14   18
    E, E, E, yes   O, O, E, yes

    11   29
    O, E, O, yes   E, O, O, yes

2.15 answer in subtraction - difference
    top number in fraction - numerator
    answer in addition - sum
    take away number in subtraction -
            subtrahend
    line in fraction - fraction bar
    number being added in addition -
            addend
    top number in subtraction -
            minuend
    bottom number in fraction -
            denominator

2.16 **Suggested Answers:**
    1 - I always do eat breakfast.
    3 - I'm not old enough to drive a car.
    1 - I have school today.
    2 - there is an equal opportunity of
       either coin falling.
    1 - of the pattern.   2, 3, 4, ...

2.17 7   6
    2,480   2,479
    $9 - 4 = 5$ $9 - 5 = 4$
    $\frac{5}{8}$ $\frac{4}{8}$
    $1.59 $1.55

Part Three

3.1 5, 0, 8, 2
    5,000, 0, 80, 2

    4, 1, 6, 3
    4,000, 100, 60, 3

3.2 =   >   =
    <   =   >
    ≠   <   =

3.3 3,677   3,776   6,377
         6,773   7,673   7,763

3.4 10 + 10 + 10 + 5,
       X + X + X + V, XXXV
    50 + 10 + 5 + 1 + 1 + 1
       L + X + V + I + I + I, LXVIII
    100 − 10 + 5 + 1,
       C − X + V + I, XCVI

3.5
    10

3.6 $\frac{4}{10}$ $\frac{3}{10}$ $\frac{2}{10}$ $\frac{1}{10}$

3.7 1 - it always does

3.8 green   yellow   orange   blue

3.9 3
    2
    1

Suggested Answers: 3.10 - 3.12

3.10 green, yellow, green, blue, yellow
    orange, green, yellow, orange, green
    4   3   2   1
    green   yellow   orange   blue
    yes

3.11 yellow, blue, yellow, green, orange
    yellow, green, blue, yellow, green
    3   4   1   2
    yellow   green   blue   orange
    no

3.12 They were close but not exactly the
    same as the probabilities.

3.13 four thousand, seventy-five - 4,075
five thousand, fifty-seven - 5,057
five thousand, five hundred seven
- 5,507
four thousand, five hundred seven
- 4,507
seven thousand, forty-five - 7,045
seven thousand, seven hundred five
- 7,705
four thousand, seven hundred
- 4,700
five thousand, seven hundred four
- 5,704

3.14 13   17   14   10   16   15

3.15 7   4   3   5   0   9

3.16 8   6   12   10   16   4

3.17 5   7   5
      8   4   9

3.18 3,459   7,063   8,547
      9,160   6,841   3,192

3.19 21   142   166   1,109   1,602
      35   26   36   129   232
      8,679   7,844   7,632   6,143
      275   205   153   244
      206   502   4,887   2,778

3.20

3.21

3.22 Suggested Answers:

3.23 cylinder — square
      cube — rectangle
      pyramid — circle
      rectangle — triangle
      solid

Part Four

4.1 1   5
     10   25
     50   100

     48¢
     76¢
     55¢
     73¢
     22¢

4.2 $ .01 $ .05 $ .10
                $ .25 $ .50 $1.00

4.3 $3 + 4 = 7, 4 + 3 = 7,$
     $7 - 3 = 4, 7 - 4 = 3$

     $5 + 5 = 10, 5 + 5 = 10,$
     $10 - 5 = 5, 10 - 5 = 5$

     $7 + 8 = 15, 8 + 7 = 15,$
     $15 - 7 = 8, 15 - 8 = 7$

     $0 + 3 = 3, 3 + 0 = 3,$
     $3 - 0 = 3, 3 - 3 = 0$

     $2 + 9 = 11, 9 + 2 = 11,$
     $11 - 2 = 9, 11 - 9 = 2$

4.4 4, 4   8, 8
     5, 5   7, 7

4.5 66, 66   153
                     $-\ 87$
                        66

     $2.74, $2.74 $5.42
                     $-\ \$2.68$
                      $2.74

     24¢, 24¢   67¢
                     $-\ 43¢$
                       24¢

     $ .81, $ .81 $1.56
                     $-\ \$\ .75$
                     $ .81

4.6 103   605   144   6,799   9,471

4.7   890
                     395   238

4.8
	142		671		931
142	95	671	296	931	397

4.9
20   20, 0
24   24, 8, 6, 9, 1, 0
148   148, 47, 38, 63, 0

4.10   20   50   90   60   50   60

4.11   300   600   400   800   600   600

4.12
90	20	300	900
+ 40	+ 80	+ 600	+ 400
124 130	99 100	899 900	1,296 1,300

4.13
40	90	600	800
− 30	− 40	− 300	− 200
14 10	46 50	268 300	565 600

4.14   200, 300, 400, 500, 600, 700, 800, 900

4.15   2,000; 3,000; 4,000; 5,000; 6,000; 7,000; 8,000; 9,000

4.16

+			
	9	12	15	11
	7	10	13	9

−			
	0	5	9	4
	1	6	10	5

4.17
122	893	1,081	7,715	5,956
28	83	154	528	2,434

4.18
379	225	657	248	417
264	649	165	338	538

4.19
6	10	16	8	2
14	12	20	4	18
5	15	35	50	20
30	10	45	40	25

4.20   LET'S EAT

Part Five

5.1   Teacher check
      Teacher check

5.2   12 + 15 > 15 + 11

5.3   6 × 2 > 5 × 2

5.4 $\frac{1}{2} = \frac{2}{4}$

5.5   50, 100, 150, 200, 250, 300, 350, 400, 450, 500

      10 hours

5.6   3, 3   0, 0
      8, 8   2, 2

5.7   413
      307
      fraction bar
      24 inches
      $7\frac{3}{5}$
      10's
      $4\frac{4}{8}$
      Suggested Answer: 7,356
      3,001

5.8   58, 77, 135, 135, 58, 77

5.9   1. Union City
      2. Riverside
      3. Madison
      4. Glen Park
      5. Littleton
      6. Jamesville

5.10 five thousand, sixty-two
      seven thousand, five hundred nine

5.11 5:15

5.12 500 cars

5.13
15 cards	23 cards	17 cards
54 books	47 books	59 books
16 shells	18 shells	26 shells

5.14 284

5.15 times   fourteen

5.16
5	10	15	20
25	30	35	40
45	50		

143

5.17 a straight line   a curved line   a closed line
Suggested Answer:

a line segment with end points   an angle

5.18

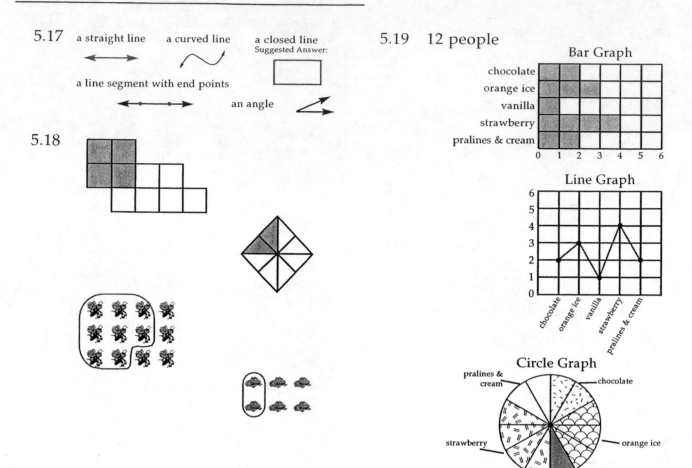

5.19 12 people

Bar Graph

Line Graph

Circle Graph

Part One

1.1 d
      f
      h
      k
      l
      g
      i
      j
      e
      b
      c
      a
      m

1.2 closed lines
     faces
     squares
     rectangles
     end points
     Angles

1.3 12, 12, 12, 12, 48
     16, 16, 16, 48

1.4 1 year = 365 days
     1 year = 365 days
     2 years = 730 days

     1 T. = 2,000 lbs.
     1 T. = 2,000 lbs.
     2 T. = 4,000 lbs.

     1 sq. yd. = 9 sq. ft.
     1 sq. yd. = 9 sq. ft.
     1 sq. yd. = 9 sq. ft.
     1 sq. yd. = 9 sq. ft.
     4 sq. yd. = 36 sq. ft.

     1 gal. = 4 qt.
     1 gal. = 4 qt.
     1 gal. = 4 qt.
     1 gal. = 4 qt.
     1 gal. = 4 qt.
     5 gal. = 20 qt.

1.5 18 18 101 162 107
     692 1,346 1,349 1,163 1,738

1.6 960 − 584 = 376   8,110 − 2,147 = 5,963   9,825 − 3,785 = 6,040
     9,029 − 4,608 = 4,421   8,379 − 5,640 = 2,739   7,161 − 4,036 = 3,125

1.7

     9, 7, +5 = 20   29 − 20 = 9   8, 9, 7, +5 = 29
     8, 8, +4 = 18   26 − 18 = 8   6, 8, 8, +4 = 26
     25, 73, +19 = 148   173 − 148 = 25   25, 56, 73, +19 = 173
     47, 88, +30 = 165   212 − 165 = 47   88, 47, 30, +47 = 212
     513, 363, +475 = 838   1,351 − 838 = 513   363, 475, +513 = 1,351
     275, 842, +356 = 1,198   1,473 − 1,198 = 275   842, 275, +356 = 1,473

145

1.8   12
      sixth
      June 23
      Wednesday, June 10
      Monday, June 22

1.9   6,374-6,376   8,638-8,640   8,999-9,001
      2,801-2,803   5,098-5,100   3,000-3,002

1.10 8   12
      31   50
      14   5
      10   30

Part Two

2.1   two-thirds   seven-eighths
      one-ninth   five-twelfths

2.2   six and three-fifths
      seven and four-eighths
      two and one-half
      four and one-third

2.3   even   even   odd
      even   even   odd

      68, blue   38, brown   121, green
      28, brown   28, red   410, orange
      147, yellow 462 blue   224, brown

2.4 $81.45
      $90.03

2.5 $\frac{5}{10}$ $\frac{1}{10}$ $\frac{7}{10}$ $\frac{3}{10}$

2.6   .5   .1   .7   .3

2.7   .3   .9   .5   .2

2.8   2,426   1,783   3,864   2,825
      2,137   3,778   2,077   2,303
      3,074   1,921   1,082   5,381

2.9   42   62   34   75   35   22
      54   21   38   16   25   48
      542   363   411   806   886
      315   413   372   156   378
      7,233   2,104   2,643   1,805

2.10 Suggested Answers:
      $ .70   2 Q, 2 D
      $ .22   2 D, 2 P
      $1.73   1 $, 2 Q, 2 D, 3P

$ .07   1 N, 2P
$3.18   3 $, 1 D, 1 N, 3 P
$ .32   3 D, 2 P

2.11 1,258; 1,260; 1,261
      7,200; 7,201; 7,203
      5,010; 5,011; 5,014

2.12 2   4   6   8
      10   12   14   16
               18   20

2.13 5   10   15   20
      25   30   35   40
               45   50

2.14 sixty-eight
      one thousand, one hundred
         forty-three
      twenty-seven
      two hundred seventy-three

2.15
30		300		900	
+70		+600		+300	
92	100	883	900	1,182	1,200
	100		600		600
	−40		−200		−400
59	60	366	400	227	200

Part Three

3.1   6, 5, 4, 0
      6,000, 500, 40, 0

      9, 0, 6, 3
      9,000, 0, 60, 3

      7, 3, 5, 1
      7,000, 300, 50, 1

3.2   3,148   3,841   4,434
               4,443   8,403   8,413

3.3   2,458   8,542   2,359   9,532
      1,379   9,731   126   6,210

3.4   6,724
      8,260
      4,081
      2,591
      1,103
      3,005

3.5 $\frac{4}{4}$ $\quad$ $\frac{2}{2}$ $\quad$ $\frac{4}{4}$

3.6 1

1

1

3.7 $3\frac{1}{2}$ inches

$2\frac{3}{4}$ inches

$4\frac{1}{4}$ inches

$1\frac{1}{2}$ inches

3.8 3, 4

2, 3

4, 5

1, 2

3.9 $4\frac{3}{5}$ $\quad$ $6\frac{4}{8}$ $\quad$ $9\frac{2}{3}$ $\quad$ $4\frac{4}{6}$

3.10 3

6

4

5

3.11

5	5	4	3	5
+9	+4	+8	+9	+5
14	9	12	12	10

5	2	9	1	5
+6	+8	+4	+9	+9
11	10	13	10	14

4	8	6	3	5
+6	+3	+6	+7	+7
10	11	12	10	12

3.12 1 $\quad$ 5

2 $\quad$ 4

1 $\quad$ 2

3.13 Teacher check

Answers to Facts

3.14

0	7	1	6	2	5	4	3
7	0	6	1	5	2	3	4

3.15 Suggested Answers:

4	5	6	7	8	9	10	11
0	1	2	3	4	5	6	7

3.16

93	171	462	778	1,130
20		177	1,221	1,281
22				
18	·	5,803	7,165	9,133
17				

3.17

5		6		
9		2		
22	36	228	537	265
2,424	4,366	1,491	837	4,947

Part Four

4.1

3	6	9	12
15	18	21	24
	27	30	

4.2

10	20	30	40
50	60	70	80
	90	100	

4.3 times $\qquad$ times

nine $\qquad$ twelve

times $\qquad$ times

thirty $\qquad$ forty

4.4 4, 8, 12, ⑯ 20, 24, 28, ㉜ 36, 40

4.5 Teacher check $\qquad$ $3\frac{1}{4}$

2

$3\frac{1}{4}$

$+2$

$10\frac{2}{4}$

Perimeter = $10\frac{2}{4}$ inches

Teacher check $\qquad$ 4

$1\frac{1}{2}$

4

$+1\frac{1}{2}$

$10\frac{2}{2} = 10 + 1 = 11$

Perimeter = 11 inches

4.6 $7\frac{4}{4} = 7 + 1 = 8$

      $5\frac{8}{8} = 5 + 1 = 6$

      $6\frac{3}{3} = 6 + 1 = 7$

      $8\frac{2}{2} = 8 + 1 = 9$

4.7

6

6

6

6

6

4.8

4.9   =   >   ≠

      <   =   <

      ≠   <   =

      >   ≠   <

4.10 $500 + 100 + 100 - 10 + 1$,

        D + C + C − X + I, DCXCI

      $100 + 50 - 10 + 1 + 1 + 1$,

        C + L − X + I + I + I, CXLIII

      $500 - 100 + 10 + 10 + 5$,

        D − C + X + X + V, CDXXV

4.11   +   ×   −   ×

      −   −   ×   +

      −   (+, −)   +   ×

      ×   −   +   +

4.12   4,000   4   400   400   40   4,000

4.13   105   143   162   1,158   832   1,275

      99

      590

      1,131

      9,172

      8,915

      4,235

      60   90

      80   40

      7,262   6,390   7,040   7,603   5,982

4.14   91   643   1,806   9,619   9,284

4.15   31   48   36   323   316   6,704

      14

      56

      286

      4,692

      1,524

      4,534

      50   30

      20   40

      6,954   4,772   3,542   3,589   3,012

4.16   37   339   345   5,058   1,376

Part Five

5.1   subtraction

5.2 $23 + ? + 27 + 22 =$

       23   93

       27   − 72

     + 22   21

       72

      21 children

5.3   4,000 pounds

      120 seconds

      48 hours

      Melinda

      April

      gallon (quart)

5.4 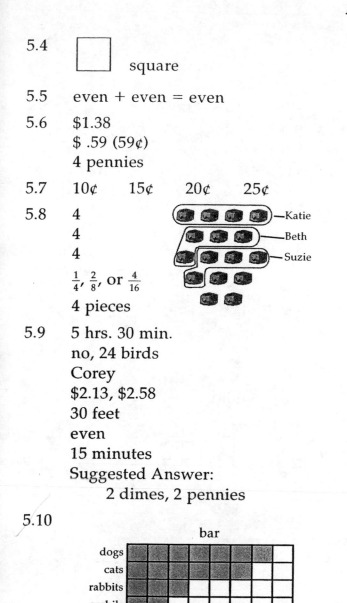 square

5.5 even + even = even

5.6 $1.38
$ .59 (59¢)
4 pennies

5.7 10¢   15¢   20¢   25¢

5.8 4
4
4
$\frac{1}{4}$, $\frac{2}{8}$, or $\frac{4}{16}$
4 pieces

—Katie
—Beth
—Suzie

5.9 5 hrs. 30 min.
no, 24 birds
Corey
$2.13, $2.58
30 feet
even
15 minutes
Suggested Answer:
   2 dimes, 2 pennies

5.10

line

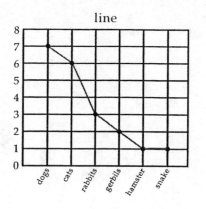

circle

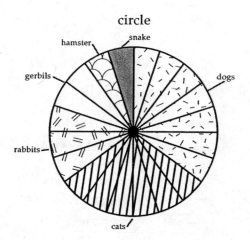

5.11 12 linear yards, 5 square yards
10 linear feet, 4 square feet

5.12 20 boxes

5.13 $10.30 $7.90 $18.20 $36.40

5.14

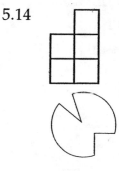

bar

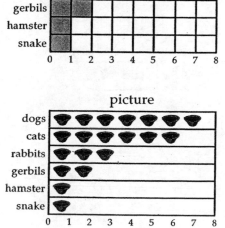

picture

Math 309 Answer Key

Part One

1.1

9	16	11	13	10	12	7	10	15
8	11	14	13	16	11	18	11	13
12	15	14	15	13	13	12	12	15

1.2

1.3

5	9	6	4	2	9	6	6	3
3	4	9	8	4	5	9	7	7
6	8	8	4	7	9	9	0	7

1.4

end points
curved line
length
line segment
straight line
angle
width
perimeter

1.5

fraction bar

numerator

denominator

1.6

three-fifths	seven-eighths
two-thirds	four-ninths
one-twelfth	one-half

1.7

$\frac{5}{8}$ $\frac{6}{7}$ $\frac{4}{10}$

$\frac{3}{5}$ $\frac{1}{3}$ $\frac{7}{12}$

1.8

one and two-thirds
five and six-sevenths
eight and one-sixth
two and three-fourths

1.9

$2\frac{1}{2}$ $9\frac{2}{3}$

$7\frac{4}{5}$ $3\frac{6}{8}$

1.10

60	60	24
30/31	12	365

1.11

addend	minuend
addend	subtrahend
sum	difference

1.12

$5 + 9 = 14$	$6 + 7 = 13$
$9 + 5 = 14$	$7 + 6 = 13$
$14 - 5 = 9$	$13 - 6 = 7$
$14 - 9 = 5$	$13 - 7 = 6$

1.13 0, 1, 2, 3, 4, 5, 6, 7, 8, 9

1.14 Suggested Answers:

1   2   3   4   5

1.15 Suggested Answers:

23   542   627   8,306   7,293

1.16 tens

57

<

place holder

1.17

1.18

1.19

150

Part Two

2.1   873   1,517   18   110   1,518
      9,260   9,161   20, 20
                             21, 21

2.2   38

2.3   83

2.4   even   even
      odd   odd

2.5

$$\begin{array}{r} 26 \\ 45 \\ +\ 372 \\ \hline 443 \end{array} \qquad \begin{array}{r} 572 \\ 39 \\ +\ 8 \\ \hline 619 \end{array} \qquad \begin{array}{r} 4,637 \\ +\ 3,294 \\ \hline 7,931 \end{array}$$

2.6   36   35   274   382   702
      2,219   4,167   5,322   2,232   159

2.7   <   <   >
      >   >   <
      <   >   >
      >   >   <
      >   <   <

2.8   5:18   7:48   1:59   3:21

2.9   32   212

2.10   40 degrees C
      70 degrees C
      80 degrees F
      180 degrees F

2.11   =   =   =
      ≠   =
      ≠   =   =
      =   =

2.12   a. north   b. east
      c. south   d. west

2.13   a. 7
      b. 8
      c. 1
      d. 2
      e. 3
      f. 5
      g. 4
      h. 6
      i. 9

2.14   +, −   −, −   (+, −), +
      +, +, −   +, −, −
      ×, +   ×, −   +, ×

2.15 $\frac{4}{5}$ $\frac{3}{7}$ $\frac{9}{12}$ $\frac{2}{2}=1$ $\frac{10}{10}=1$ $\frac{8}{8}=1$

      $6\frac{2}{3}$ $11\frac{5}{6}$ $5\frac{6}{9}$ $13\frac{8}{11}$ $8\frac{4}{4}=8+1=9$ $12\frac{6}{6}=12+1=13$

2.16   3 yards, 1 yard, 8 yards
      5 feet, 4 feet, 18 feet

2.17   30, 20, 30, 10, 35

2.18   NS
      NS
      S
      NS

Part Three

3.1   30, 25, 35, 40, 40

3.2   a. 5
      b. 1
      c. 4
      d. 3
      e. 2

3.3   6   7   4
      8   9
      27   43
      64

3.4   4:08 AM   7:35 PM   12:50 PM   9:12 AM

3.5   minutes, hour
      AM, PM

3.6   14   6   18   4
      12   10   2   20
              8   16

      25   50   30   45
      15   40   20   5
             10   35

3.7   nickel   penny   quarter   dime

3.8   12   36
      3   5,280
      144   9

| 3.9 | 62 | 128 | 650 | 1,414 | 1,443 |
| | 7,121 | 7,337 | 8,257 | 9,524 | 6,919 |

3.10 ├────────────┤

3.11 8 square feet
10 square yards

3.12	30	10	90	40
	20	70	80	60
		50	100	

3.13 $\frac{2}{4}$ $\frac{4}{6}$ $\frac{2}{10}$ $\frac{3}{9}$ $\frac{7}{12}$ $\frac{8}{15}$
$4\frac{1}{9}$ $5\frac{1}{4}$ $3\frac{3}{7}$ $3\frac{1}{3}$ $2\frac{7}{12}$ $4\frac{2}{8}$

| 3.14 | 26 | 62 | 246 | 462 |
| | 642 | 2,436 | 4,364 | 4,634 |

| 3.15 | 36 | 15 | 124 | 114 | 418 |
| | 3,463 | 2,745 | 3,807 | 1,054 | 7,008 |

3.16 6, 2, 4, 3, 8

3.17	15	30	9	12
	6	24	3	27
		18	21	
	12	32	20	4
	24	28	8	32
		40	36	

3.18 7, 8, 0, 3
7,000, 800, 0, 3

5, 2, 3, 9
5,000, 200, 30, 9

0, 6, 4, 1
0, 600, 40, 1

| 3.19 | tens | thousands | thousands |
| | hundreds | tens | ones |

3.20 three thousand, two hundred
fifty-four
four thousand, sixty-five
five thousand, four
eight thousand, five hundred two

3.21 4,156
9,140
6,073
1,008

Part Four

| 4.1 | 16 | 2,000 | 12 |

4.2	11	12
	5	70
	40	10
	54	25
	63	42

| 4.3 | + | × | < | ≠ or < |
| | = | − | > | + |

4.4
```
    9            763
    8            529
   17          + 38
 + 24          1,330
 ───
   58
```
```
             16          2,365
             23        + 5,037
             55          7,402
           + 48
           ────
            142
```

| 4.5 | 3,000 | 4,000 | 6,000 |
| | 3,000 | 8,000 | 8,000 |

| 4.6 | 8,000 | 9,000 | 3,000 |
| | 3,000 | 6,000 | 5,000 |

4.7	60	60	40
	40	90	80
	400	500	300

4.8 Suggested Answers:
1, I always do
2, I eat pizza once in a while
3, no one has flown to Mars
3, we usually go to the beach
2, there is an equal opportunity to
pick black or blue
3, there are many more blue marbles
than black marbles

4.9 8, 7
9,000
gallon
15
7, 4

4.10 16   2
2   4

4.11 gallon feet
miles pounds
hours inches

4.12 Suggested answers:

cereal gram ounce
liquid soap liter quart
margarine grams pound

4.13

Y
Y
N
Y
Y
N

4.14 4, 2, 3, 6, 5

4.14 100 + 100 + 50 + 5 + 1 + 1 + 1
C + C + L + V + I + I + I,
CCLVIII

500 + 100 + 100 + 100 + 10 + 5 − 1,
D + C + C + C + X + V − 1,
DCCCXIV
1,000 + 1,000 + 1,
M + M + I, MMI

4.16 C + C + L − X + V
100 + 100 + 50 − 10 + 5; 245
D + C + L + X − I
500 + 100 + 50 + 10 − 1; 659
M + M + V, 1,000 + 1,000 + 5; 2,005

4.17

72	367	9,406	4,351
− 45	− 192	− 5,362	− 2,670
27	175	4,044	1,681

4.18 12   730
6,000 60
12   8

Part Five

5.1 I II III IV V
VI VII VIII IX X

5.2 12 minutes

5.3 60 minutes

5.4 $4.52
Suggested Answer:
4 dollars, 2 quarters, 2 pennies

5.5 435
6,905
six thousand, nine hundred five

5.6 5 > 4
7 < 9
8 < 15
31 > 30

5.7 65¢ + 38¢ + 38¢ = 141¢ or $1.41
15 + 21 = 36 days
63 − 59 = 4 ants
124 − 98 = 26 pages

5.8 70
600
7,000

5.9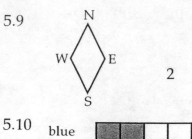

2

5.10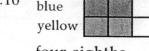
blue
yellow

four-eighths

$$+ \frac{2}{8}$$ over $\frac{2}{8}$ equals $\frac{4}{8}$

5.11 a. 5
      b. 1
      c. 4
      d. 3
      e. 2

5.12 linear
      square

5.13 Thursday, Wednesday, Friday
          Monday, Tuesday
      Monday, Tuesday

5.14 Suggested Answer:
      Jason bought a soda for 47¢ and a
      hamburger for $2.55. He spent
      $3.02 altogether. He paid $4.00.
      His change was 98¢.

5.15 Patty, Susie, Jennifer, Kevin, Mike

5.16 2   5   8   5
      6   4   10
      43   49   37
      13   275

5.17

5.18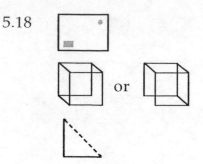

5.19 Team Home Runs
      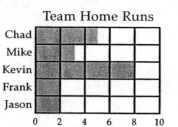

Part One

1.1   20, 30, 40, 50, 60, 70, 80, 90
       200, 300, 400, 500, 600, 700, 800, 900

1.2   50   70   80   200   600   900

1.3
90	80	500	700
+40	+80	+500	+200
128 130	160 160	994 1,000	857 900

70	60	800	400
−50	−20	−500	−200
24 20	36 40	277 300	215 200

1.4   10 + 20 + 30 + 20 = 80 plates
       200 + 300 + 400 = 900 people

1.5   2,000; 3,000; 4,000; 5,000;
       6,000; 7,000; 8,000; 9,000

1.6   5,000   8,000   9,000   1,000

1.7
5,000	2,000	3,000
+2,000	+3,000	+4,000
6,965 7,000	4,603 5,000	7,223 7,000

6,000	9,000	3,000
−2,000	−5,000	−1,000
3,541 4,000	4,385 4,000	1,885 2,000

1.8   3,000; 2,000; 4,000; 9,000 people
       2,000; 2,000; 4,000; 8,000 miles

1.9   11   22   105   193   1,072

       6,018   7,957   7,143   8,120
       7,803   5,655   9,585   8,056

1.10 $\frac{3}{4}$ $\frac{7}{8}$ $\frac{5}{7}$ $\frac{6}{8}$
                                    $\frac{5}{12}$

       $\frac{3}{3} = 1$ $\frac{5}{5} = 1$ $\frac{6}{6} = 1$ $\frac{9}{9} = 1$
                                         $\frac{2}{2} = 1$

1.11   38   186   349   567   239

       2,175   569   6,152   2,504
       3,508   5,109   1,906   2,768

1.12 $\frac{4}{8}$ $\frac{2}{7}$ $\frac{2}{5}$ $\frac{1}{6}$
                                    $\frac{5}{12}$

       $\frac{5}{10}$ $\frac{3}{9}$ $\frac{1}{4}$ $\frac{1}{3}$
                                    $\frac{2}{8}$

1.13   2, 4, 6, 8, 10, 12, 14, 16, 18, 20
       3, 6, 9, 12, 15, 18, 21, 24, 27, 30
       4, 8, 12, 16, 20, 24, 28, 32, 36, 40
       5, 10, 15, 20, 25, 30, 35, 40, 45, 50
       10, 20, 30, 40, 50, 60, 70, 80, 90, 100

1.14   3 + 7 = 10   4 + 9 = 13   7 + 8 = 15
       7 + 3 = 10   9 + 4 = 13   8 + 7 = 15
       10 − 3 = 7   13 − 4 = 9   15 − 7 = 8
       10 − 7 = 3   13 − 9 = 4   15 − 8 = 7

1.15   10   6   13   12   8   11

1.16   60   60   24
       30/31   12   365

Part Two

2.1   THAT BIRD IS IN A HURRY!

2.2   12   36
       3   5,280
       144   9

2.3   18   22   14
       3   7   8
       14   7   39
       60   60

2.4   ⑯   2   15   1
             1   ②   2   1
             1   ㊶   1   42
       ㊲   2   67   ㊾   2

2.5   numerator
       fraction bar
                     denominator

2.6 $\frac{4}{8}$ four-eighths
       $\frac{1}{4}$ one-fourth
       $2\frac{1}{3}$ two and one-third
       $\frac{3}{8}$ three-eighths
       $3\frac{5}{8}$ three and five-eighths
       $3\frac{2}{3}$ three and two-thirds
       $4\frac{1}{2}$ four and one-half
       $2\frac{3}{8}$ two and three-eighths

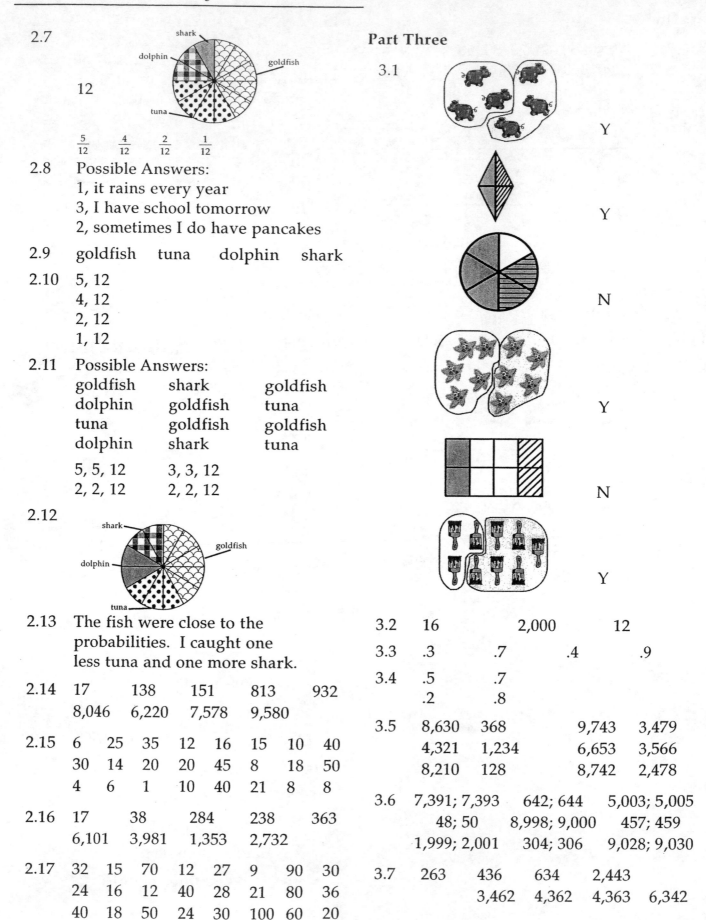

2.7

12

$\frac{5}{12}$ $\frac{4}{12}$ $\frac{2}{12}$ $\frac{1}{12}$

2.8 Possible Answers:
1, it rains every year
3, I have school tomorrow
2, sometimes I do have pancakes

2.9 goldfish tuna dolphin shark

2.10 5, 12
4, 12
2, 12
1, 12

2.11 Possible Answers:

goldfish shark goldfish
dolphin goldfish tuna
tuna goldfish goldfish
dolphin shark tuna

5, 5, 12 3, 3, 12
2, 2, 12 2, 2, 12

2.12

2.13 The fish were close to the probabilities. I caught one less tuna and one more shark.

2.14 17 138 151 813 932
8,046 6,220 7,578 9,580

2.15 6 25 35 12 16 15 10 40
30 14 20 20 45 8 18 50
4 6 1 10 40 21 8 8

2.16 17 38 284 238 363
6,101 3,981 1,353 2,732

2.17 32 15 70 12 27 9 90 30
24 16 12 40 28 21 80 36
40 18 50 24 30 100 60 20

Part Three

3.1

Y

Y

N

Y

N

Y

3.2 16 2,000 12

3.3 .3 .7 .4 .9

3.4 .5 .7
.2 .8

3.5 8,630 368 9,743 3,479
4,321 1,234 6,653 3,566
8,210 128 8,742 2,478

3.6 7,391; 7,393 642; 644 5,003; 5,005
48; 50 8,998; 9,000 457; 459
1,999; 2,001 304; 306 9,028; 9,030

3.7 263 436 634 2,443
3,462 4,362 4,363 6,342

3.8
$\frac{4}{5}$ $\frac{7}{7}=1$ $\frac{7}{9}$ $\frac{2}{8}$ $\frac{2}{6}$ $\frac{3}{10}$
$\frac{2}{3}$ $\frac{5}{6}$ $\frac{10}{10}=1$ $\frac{3}{7}$ $\frac{2}{12}$ $\frac{1}{4}$
$7\frac{3}{7}$ $8\frac{3}{3}=8+1=9$ $11\frac{2}{2}=11+1=12$ $5\frac{4}{4}=5+1=6$
$2\frac{2}{4}$ $4\frac{1}{5}$ $7\frac{2}{10}$ $4\frac{6}{12}$

3.9 16   2
     2   4

3.10 six   nine
      plus   times
      equals   Seven
      sixteen   thirteen
      Eight   seven

3.11 16 linear feet
      16 square feet

      12 linear yards
      6 square yards

3.12 Suggested Answers:
      ounce   quart
      pound (ounce) feet
      pound (ounce) gallon

3.13 cup   pint   quart   gallon

3.14
71
  24
+ 73
  97
168
− 97
  71

80
  57
+ 94
 151
231
− 151
  80

79
  89
+ 26
 115
194
− 115
  79

551
 434
+ 275
 709
1,260
− 709
  551

179
 285
+ 463
 748
927
− 748
 179

263
 402
+ 378
 780
1,043
− 780
  263

3.15
81
  32
+ 49
  81
92
  27
+ 65
  92
56
  19
+ 37
  56

18
  61
− 43
  18
15
  74
− 59
  15
19
  47
− 28
  19

3.16 thirteen
      forty-seven
      four hundred thirty-nine
      seven hundred six
      four thousand, eight hundred two
      seven thousand, fifty-four

3.17 734
      401
      8,291
      5,742
      9,761
      5,348

3.18 63¢ ($ .63)
      $1.25
      $3.16
      38¢ ($ .38)

Part Four

4.1 4:15   8:20   1:47   10:13

4.2

4.3 30   90   80   40
     300   700   400   500
     4,000 9,000 2,000 6,000

4.4 72   8
     120   72
     6,000 10,560
     24   48

157

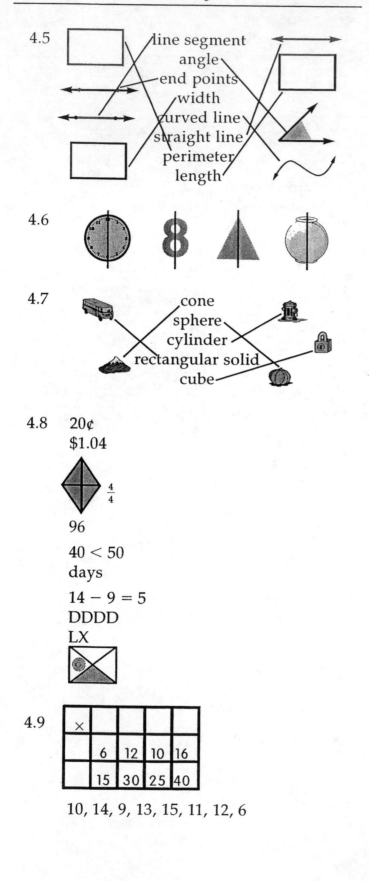

4.5 line segment / angle / end points / width / curved line / straight line / perimeter / length

4.6

4.7 cone / sphere / cylinder / rectangular solid / cube

4.8 20¢
$1.04

$\frac{4}{4}$

96

40 < 50
days

14 − 9 = 5
DDDD
LX

4.9

×				
	6	12	10	16
	15	30	25	40

10, 14, 9, 13, 15, 11, 12, 6

4.10 500 + 100 + 50 − 10 + 1 + 1,
    D + C + L − X + I + I, DCXLII
1,000 + 500 + 100 + 100 + 100 +
50 + 1 + 1,
    M + D + C + C + C + L + I + I,
MDCCCLII

4.11 D + C + C + X + V,
    500 + 100 + 100 + 10 + 5, 715
M + M − C + L,
    1,000 + 1,000 − 100 + 50, 1,950

4.12 0, 4, 0, 5
0, 400, 0, 5

6, 3, 4, 1
6,000, 300, 40, 1

2, 3, 5, 4
2,000, 300, 50, 4

4.13 ones, 3   tens, 0
thousands, 4,000   hundreds, 300

4.14 90
80
40
50

4.15 156   149   882   1,163   1,273
6,601   8,914   9,851   7,694

4.16 455   216   315   19   504
4,899   6,413   3,573   5,502
5,015   3,834   2,387   1,962

4.17

$\frac{1}{3}$ $+\frac{1}{3}$ = $\frac{2}{3}$ $\frac{3}{6}$ $+\frac{1}{6}$ = $\frac{4}{6}$ $\frac{4}{9}$ $-\frac{3}{9}$ = $\frac{1}{9}$ $\frac{6}{12}$ $-\frac{2}{12}$ = $\frac{4}{12}$

4.18

$3\frac{1}{4}$ $+2\frac{2}{4}$ = $5\frac{3}{4}$ $6\frac{2}{8}$ $+4\frac{5}{8}$ = $10\frac{7}{8}$ $4\frac{7}{10}$ $-1\frac{5}{10}$ = $3\frac{2}{10}$ $7\frac{4}{5}$ $-6\frac{3}{5}$ = $1\frac{1}{5}$

4.19 Suggested Answers:
$\frac{2}{2}$ $\frac{3}{3}$ $\frac{4}{4}$ $\frac{5}{5}$ $\frac{6}{6}$ $\frac{7}{7}$

Part Five

5.1 $3 + 2 + 1 = 5 + 1$
$\qquad 6 = 6$
or $3 + 2 = 5 + 1 - 1$
$\qquad 5 = 5$

$9 + 6 - 4 = 7 + 4$
$\qquad 11 = 11$
or $9 + 6 = 7 + 4 + 4$
$\qquad 15 = 15$

$18 - 9 + 5 = 6 + 8$
$\qquad 14 = 14$
or $18 - 9 = 6 + 8 - 5$
$\qquad 9 = 9$

$7 + 8 + 1 = 12 + 4$
$\qquad 16 = 16$
or $7 + 8 = 12 + 4 - 1$
$\qquad 15 = 15$

$5 + 2 - 1 = 14 - 8$
$\qquad 6 - 6$
or $5 + 2 = 14 - 8 + 1$
$\qquad 7 = 7$

$12 - 3 + 4 = 4 + 9$
$\qquad 13 = 13$
or $12 - 3 = 4 + 9 - 4$
$\qquad 9 = 9$

5.2 $15 - 7, 8$ $\qquad 8 + 3, 11$ $\qquad 7 - 3, 4$
$13 - 5, 8$ $\qquad 6 + 4, 10$ $\qquad 5 + 9, 14$
$47 - 9, 38$ $\qquad 28 + 2, 30$ $\qquad 70 - 20, 50$

5.3 4 flowers
2 cookies
4 tickets

5.4 10 linear inches
6 square inches

12 linear inches
6 square inches

14 linear inches
6 inches

no, yes
more sides showing
use the same number of square
$\qquad$ units each time
no, no

5.5 Suggested Answers:

12 linear inches
8 square inches

14 linear inches
8 square inches

16 linear inches
8 square inches

no, yes
12 linear inches, 16 linear inches

5.6 213
east
Friday
134
5 yrs, 12 yrs, 8 yrs

5.7 $\frac{6}{6}$
$\frac{2}{6}$
$\frac{4}{6}$
$\frac{2}{6}$
$\frac{2}{6}$
$\frac{1}{6}$

5.8 3, 6, 9, 12, 15, 18, 21, 24, 27, 30
4, 8, 12, 16, 20, 24, 28, 32, 36, 40

5.9 one hour
gallons
miles
cups (glasses)
dollars

5.10 second
ninth
sixteenth
twentieth

5.11	3,060	5,000	2,010	6,100
5.12	XI	V	IX	
	VI	VII	V	
	XII	VIII	X	

Part One

1.01 8   9   7   4   13   14   6   10
      5   4   6   7   7   4   5   8

1.02 0, 1, 2, 3, 4, 5, 6, 7, 8, 9

1.03 12   35   41   47   67   73   76   93

1.04 thirteen   forty-seven
      sixty-three   twenty
      eight   ninety-five

Part Two

2.01 5, 8   3, 0
      50, 8   30, 0

2.02 74, seventy-four
      69, sixty-nine

2.03   addend   minuend
      +   addend   −   subtrahend
      79   sum   17 difference

2.04 68   85   79   34   23   27

2.05 14   15
      8   4

Part Three

3.01 252   352   452   552
             652   752   852   952

3.02 498, 500   300, 302   751, 753

3.03 5, 0, 7
      500, 0, 7

3.04 six hundred thirty-one
      one hundred three

3.05 479   15   623   560

3.06 yards
      feet
      inches
      dozen

Part Four

4.01 $6 + 5 = 11$
      $18 - 9 \neq 7$

4.02 ≠   =
      >   <

4.03 35   54   92   52   160

4.04 sixth
      third

4.05 12, 7
      30, 31
      29

4.06 3:55   8:19

Part Five

5.01 91
      803
      eight hundred three

5.02 $76 < 95$

5.03 15   0

5.04 12   36

5.05 inches

5.06 35 rocks
      23 rocks

5.07 198   82
      33   440

Math 302 Self Test Key

Part One

1.01 6 + 7, 13   13 − 6, 7   13 − 7, 6
      17 − 9, 8   8 + 9, 17   9 + 8, 17

1.02 39, 40, 41
      yes

1.03 39   96   479   998   11
      93   53   61   91   74
      55   51   326   732   440

Part Two

2.01 900, 0
      place holder

2.02 8, 6, 3   4, 7, 9
      800, 60, 3   400, 70, 9

2.03   56
        + 42
        ____
          98

2.04 0   0, 5
      0, 2, 4, 6, 8

2.05 five hundred eight
      fifty-eight

2.06 806   926   721   980

Part Three

3.01 22, 24   even
      49, 51   odd

3.02   numerator
      fraction bar
                    denominator

3.03 two-fifths

3.04

3.05 28   68   15   58   44

3.06 <   >
      =   ≠

3.07 five hundred ninety-three

Part Four

4.01 triangle
      flat
      circle

4.02 121¢, $1.21
      110¢, $1.10

4.03 15   978   979

4.04 56   17   46

Part Five

5.01 ones, 5   tens, 50
      hundreds, 900   hundreds, 800

5.02 12   36   3
      Thursday

5.03 Sixty-nine plus twenty-eight is not
         equal to eighty-seven.
      Fourteen minus eight is less than
         four plus six.

5.04 41 cars
      5 cars

5.05   378   95
        + 463   − 47
        _____   ____
          841   48

Part One

1.01 $7 + 8 = 15, 8 + 7 = 15$
$15 - 7 = 8, 15 - 8 = 7$

1.02 addend
addend
sum

1.03 372   809

1.04 89   133   101   108
103   188   894   885
876   642   915   717

Part Two

2.01 pound   quart
gallon   ounce

2.02 16   2,000
16   2
2   4

2.03 $4 + 8 = 12, 8 + 4 = 12$
$12 - 4 = 8, 12 - 8 = 4$
$7 + 7 = 14, 7 + 7 = 14$
$14 - 7 = 7, 14 - 7 = 7$
$9 + 0 = 9, 0 + 9 = 9$
$9 - 0 = 9, 9 - 9 = 0$

2.04 356   653

2.05 744   873   943   122

Part Three

3.01 16   58   218   724

3.02 382   364   272   572

3.03 $6 > 4$
$15 + 14 \neq 20 + 15$

3.04

$\frac{7}{8}$ $\frac{3}{5}$ $\frac{1}{2}$

7:18

Part Four

4.01 $\frac{2}{6}$ $\frac{2}{5}$

4.02 $\frac{6}{6}$ $\frac{5}{5}$

4.03 midnight
noon
A.M.

4.04 hundreds, 300   ones, 4
ones, 7   tens, 90

4.05 14   107   137   958   602
734   922   989   652   733

Part Five

5.01 $2 + 8 = 10, 8 + 2 = 10$
$10 - 2 = 8, 10 - 8 = 2$
$0 + 4 = 4, 4 + 0 = 4$
$4 - 0 = 4, 4 - 4 = 0$

5.02 $ .74 $3.09

5.03 112   792   756   7   303   162

5.04 $34 + 29 = 63$
$34 > 29$

5.05 $\frac{4}{6}$
$\frac{2}{6}$ $\frac{6}{6}$

5.06

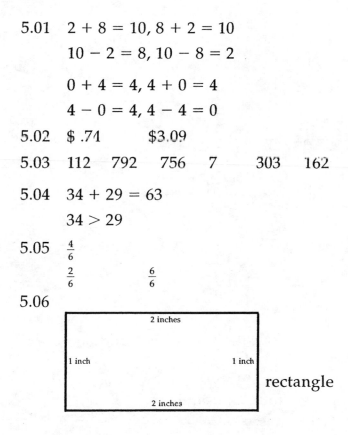

rectangle

163

Math 304 Self Test Key

Part One

1.01 hundreds   ones
      thousands   tens

1.02 8,072

1.03 1,034   1,035   1,036   1,037   1,038

1.04 15   19
     18   11

1.05 1,033   836   1,079
     707   1,108

Part Two

2.01

$$60 + 40 \\ \underline{} \\ 99 \quad 100$$

$$70 + 40 \\ \underline{} \\ 108 \quad 110$$

2.02 18   55   578   156   132   485

2.03 $1\frac{1}{2}$

$2\frac{1}{4}$

2.04 12   60   16
     12   2   3

2.05 Suggested Answers:
     L   W
     V
     T

Part Three

3.01 four thousand, six hundred
       ninety-two
    eight thousand, sixty-one
    four thousand, six

3.02 6, 7, 4, 9
     6,000, 700, 40, 9

3.03 6,378; 6,380   7,999; 8,001   6,118; 6,120

3.04 Suggested Answers:
     4   3   3
     4   7   1   3

3.05 <   <   >
     =   ≠   =

3.06

$$523 \\ 42 \\ \underline{+\ 18} \\ 583$$

$$548 \\ \underline{-\ 432} \\ 116$$

Part Four

4.01 10, 5, 1, 1, 17

4.02

4.03 3, 6, 9, 12, 15, 18, 21, 24, 27, 30

4.04

$\frac{4}{9} + \frac{2}{9} = \frac{6}{9}$

$\frac{7}{8} - \frac{3}{8} = \frac{4}{8}$

4.05 14   105   880   920
     7   46   238   468

Part Five

5.01 7 + 8 = 15, 8 + 7 = 15
     15 − 7 = 8, 15 − 8 = 7

5.02 0, 1, 2, 3, 4, 5, 6, 7, 8, 9

5.03 0
     place holder

5.04 70   100

5.05 five thousand, eight hundred four

5.06 three-eighths   seven-ninths

5.07 $\frac{5}{12}$ box of cookies

5.08

$$52 \\ 45 \\ \underline{+\ 8} \\ 105$$

$$721 \\ 46 \\ \underline{+\ 8} \\ 775$$

$$52 \\ \underline{-\ 5} \\ 47$$

$$346 \\ \underline{-\ 72} \\ 274$$

Part One

1.01
3,508   3,510
3,506   3,507   ~~3,580~~   3,509   ~~3,501~~   3,511

1.02   ⑥   1<u>5</u>   497   ⑯⑫   357   ⑴,⑸⑻⑷
      ones   hundreds   thousands

1.03   ✎   121   85   ●   37   78

$$121 \quad \begin{array}{r} 85 \\ +\ 36 \\ \hline 121 \end{array} \qquad \begin{array}{r} 78 \\ -\ 41 \\ \hline 37 \end{array} \quad 37$$

1.04   51   1,197   1,022   17   325   238

1.05

forty-third	13
seventy-sixth	32
thirteenth	43
sixty-eighth	17
thirty-second	68
seventeenth	76

(forty-third → 43, seventy-sixth → 76, thirteenth → 13, sixty-eighth → 68, thirty-second → 32, seventeenth → 17)

1.06 $\frac{3}{5}$ $\frac{6}{7}$ $\frac{3}{8}$ $\frac{2}{9}$

Part Two

2.01   5, 0, 6, 3
5,000, 0, 60, 3

2.02   1,221   1,371   369   275

2.03   78   32   212

2.04

Temperature in Degrees F.

	0	20	40	60	80	100	120	140	160	180	200	220
inside												
outside												

2.05   Twenty-six plus thirty-five is not equal to fifty-one.
Nine plus three is greater than seven plus four.
Seventeen minus nine is less than eight plus six.

Part Three

3.01

$$\begin{array}{r} 300 \\ +\ 300 \\ \hline 600 \end{array} \quad 621 \qquad \begin{array}{r} 400 \\ +\ 400 \\ \hline 800 \end{array} \quad 783$$

3.02 $2\frac{1}{2}$ $3\frac{1}{4}$

3.03   2, 1, 2, 1, 6

3.04   Lines of symmetry may vary.

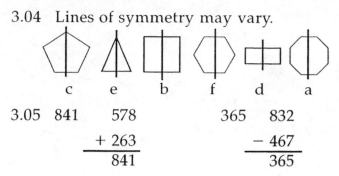

     c   e   b   f   d   a

3.05

$$841 \quad \begin{array}{r} 578 \\ +\ 263 \\ \hline 841 \end{array} \qquad 365 \quad \begin{array}{r} 832 \\ -\ 467 \\ \hline 365 \end{array}$$

Part Four

4.01   even   odd

4.02   14   11
O, O, E, yes   O, E, O, yes

4.03   3,650   7,049

4.04   597   843   422   378

4.05   X + V − I, 10 + 5 − 1, 14
X + X + V − I, 10 + 10 + 5 − 1, 24

4.06 $\frac{6}{7}$ $\frac{5}{6}$ $\frac{3}{12}$ $\frac{3}{9}$

Part Five

5.01   399   XIII

5.02   Suggested Answers:
1 dollar, 8 dimes, 1 penny
1 dollar, 3 nickels, 2 pennies

5.03   70   400

5.04   14 seconds
4 months

5.05   Five hundred nine minus two hundred eleven is equal to two hundred ninety-eight.
Four plus eight is greater than three plus seven.

5.06 $\frac{5}{8}$ $\frac{3}{8}$ $\frac{3}{10}$ $\frac{7}{10}$

$$\begin{array}{r} \frac{2}{8} \\ +\ \\ \hline \frac{5}{8} \end{array} \qquad\qquad \begin{array}{r} \frac{4}{10} \\ -\ \\ \hline \frac{3}{10} \end{array}$$

Math 306 Self Test Key

Part One

1.01 6,673   7,843   4,531   6,226

1.02 2, 4, 6, 8, 10, 12, 14, 16, 18, 20
3, 6, 9, 12, 15, 18, 21, 24, 27, 30

1.03 58   87
O, O, E, yes   O, E, O, yes

1.04 even
odd
12

1.05 hour
second

1.06 60   60   24
30/31   12   365

Part Two

2.01 14   246   184   166   2,334

2.02 12   36
3   5,280
144   9

2.03 16 linear feet, 15 square feet

2.04

$$\begin{array}{cccc}
\frac{2}{7} & \frac{5}{12} & \frac{8}{10} & \frac{9}{16} \\
+\ \frac{3}{7} & +\ \frac{6}{12} & -\ \frac{4}{10} & -\ \frac{3}{16} \\
\hline
\frac{5}{7} & \frac{11}{12} & \frac{4}{10} & \frac{6}{16}
\end{array}$$

2.05 356   6,530   145   5,410
place holder

2.06   ≠   <   >

Part Three

3.01 5,542   9,232   677   2,325

3.02 $\frac{1}{2} = \frac{2}{4}$

3.03 $\frac{1}{2} = \frac{2}{4}$

3.04 $2.28
+ $ .35
$2.63

3.05 L + X + V − 1, 50 + 10 + 5 − 1, 64
M + C + C + X,
1,000 + 100 + 100 + 10, 1,210

3.06   70   500
+ 40   + 400
107   110   906   900

Part Four

4.01 2   4   6   8
10   12   14   16
18   20

4.02

Cars

4.03

4.04 4 + 6 ≠ 11
95 > 76

4.05 70   4.06   3,352
6,840

Part Five

5.01

$$\begin{array}{c}
\frac{6}{8} \\
-\ \frac{3}{8} \\
\hline
\frac{3}{8}
\end{array}$$

5.02 $2.06

5.03 144

5.04 356,   4,   8,492,   650,   408

5.05 nine thousand, sixty-three

5.06 60   60   24
30/31   12   365

5.07 year, month, date, day

5.08 Sunday

5.09 multiples of 2, or even numbers to 20

Part One

1.01 Suggested Answers:
4   258   76

1.02 5   10   15   20
25   30   35   40
45   50

1.03 three-fourths
five-twelfths
four and one-third
six and two-fifths
two and four-eighths
seven and four-sixths

1.04 6,865   5,860   6,196   1,042

1.05 288   569   2,378   3,858

Part Two

2.01 12   36
5,280   3
144   9

2.02 18 linear inches, 11 square inches

2.03 $7\frac{3}{5}$ $5\frac{2}{8}$

2.04 43   44
O, E, O, yes   E, E, E, yes

2.05 6,259   1,469   145   362

Part Three

3.01 10 + 10 + 10 − 1,
X + X + X − I, XXIX
50 + 10 + 10 + 10 + 1,
L + X + X + X + I, LXXXI

3.02

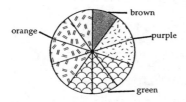

3.03 1, 2, 3, 4

3.04

3.05 Suggested Answer:

3.06 8,209   8,955   538   4,867

Part Four

4.01 86, 86   134 $4.42, $4.42 $7.65
                − 48   − $3.23
                ───   ──────
                 86                    $4.42

4.02 125   72   663   295

4.03 46¢
18¢
67¢

4.04   80   300   90   500
      +30   +500   −20   −300
      ──────   ──────   ─────   ──────
      108 110   822 800   64 70   229 200

4.05 338   2,159

4.06 6   10   5   20

Part Five

5.01 9 + 8 < 7 + 11

5.02 Judy's brother

5.03 six

5.04 $3\frac{6}{8}$

5.05 24 students
21 students
28 students

5.06 4,036

5.07   Suggested Answer:

5.08 3 feet

5.09

brown
(chocolate)

yellow
(vanilla)

167

Math 308 Self Test Key

Part One

1.01 faces, squares, end points

1.02 48

	1 ft	12 in
	1 ft	12 in
	1 ft	12 in
	1 ft	12 in
	4 ft	= 48 in

32

	1 lb	16 oz
	1 lb	16 oz
	2 lb	= 32 oz

25

1 nickel	5 pennies
1 nickel	5 pennies
1 nickel	5 pennies
1 nickel	5 pennies
1 nickel	5 pennies
5 nickel =	25 pennies

1.03 45

$$76 + 38 = 114$$

$$159 - 114 = 45$$

$$76 + 38 + 45 = 159$$

159

$$387 + 246 = 633$$

$$792 - 633 = 159$$

$$387 + 246 + 159 = 792$$

1.04 third

1.05 5,166; 5,168   9,637; 9,639   7,999; 8,001

1.06 0   47
      12   50

Part Two

2.01 mixed number, two and one-fifth
      fraction, three-fourths

2.02 99   odd, even, odd

2.03 .3, three-tenths

2.04 38   287   616   4,635   1,647

2.05 $1.27   1$, 2 D, 1 N, 2P

2.06

$$400 + 300 = 705 \quad 700$$

$$900 - 600 = 343 \quad 300$$

2.07 two hundred sixty-eight

Part Three

3.01 7, 6, 0, 9
      7,000, 600, 0, 9

3.02 8,003   4,307

3.03 $5\frac{3}{5}$ $6\frac{4}{8}$ $10\frac{7}{9}$ $7\frac{2}{2} = 7+1 = 8$ $4\frac{4}{4} = 4+1 = 5$

3.04 3, 2, 8, 9

3.05

9	●	●	●	●	●	
10	●	●	●	●		
0	1	2	3	4	5	

Part Four

4.01

3	6	10	20
9	12	30	40
	15	50	

4.02 a. length $2\frac{1}{2}''$ $2\frac{1}{2}$
      b. width $1''$ 1

$$2\frac{1}{2}$$
$$1$$
$$6\frac{2}{2} = 6 + 1 = 7 \text{ inches}$$

4.03

4.04 $500 + 50 - 10 + 5 + 1 + 1$
      D + L − X + V + I + I, DXLVII

4.05 6,897   1,391   487   2,867

Part Five

5.01 18, 24, 13, 63   8 birds

5.02 1 dollar, 1 dime, 1 nickel, 3 pennies

5.03 8 tops

5.04 14 linear yards, 6 square yards

5.05 42 linear feet

5.06

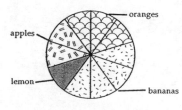

Part One

1.01   14   10   15   16   11
       6   2   5   7   6

1.02

1.03 length
      line segment
      perimeter
      end points
      angle

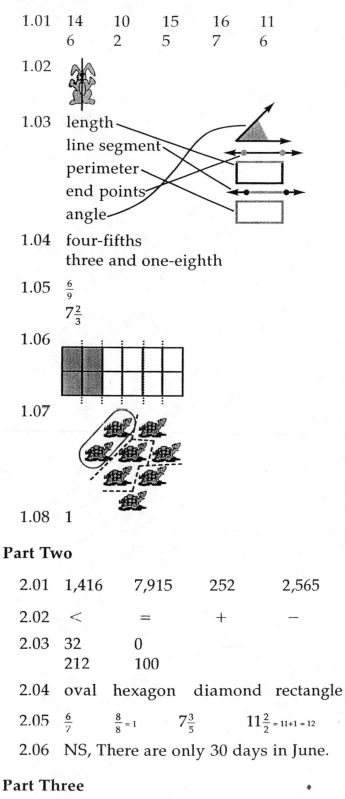

1.04 four-fifths
      three and one-eighth

1.05 $\frac{6}{9}$
      $7\frac{2}{3}$

1.06

1.07

1.08 1

Part Two

2.01 1,416   7,915   252   2,565

2.02 <   =   +   −

2.03 32   0
      212   100

2.04 oval hexagon diamond rectangle

2.05 $\frac{6}{7}$ $\frac{8}{8}=1$ $7\frac{3}{5}$ $11\frac{2}{2}=11+1=12$

2.06 NS, There are only 30 days in June.

Part Three

3.01 cube pyramid cylinder cone

3.02 12   12   27   25
      20   24   5   40
             20   28

3.03 7 square feet

3.04 $\frac{3}{8}$ $2\frac{3}{6}$

3.05 4, 6, 2, 1
      4,000, 600, 20, 1

3.06 tens   7,085

3.07 two thousand, seventy

Part Four

4.01 367   4,639   894   4,006
      482   + 307   − 57   − 2,381
    + 32   4,946   837   1,625
     881

4.02 5,000   5,000   9,000

4.03 mile   ounce

4.04   Y

4.05 16
      3

4.06 500 + 100 + 100 + 50 − 10 + 5 + 1,
      D + C + C + L − X + V + I,
      DCCXLVI
      M + M + V + I + I,
      1,000 + 1,000 + 5 + 1 + 1,
      2,007

4.07 15   8

Part Five

5.01 $6.14
      Suggested Answer:
           6 dollars, 1 dime, 4 pennies

5.02 9,304
      nine thousand, three hundred four

5.03 800
      5,000

5.04 $\frac{4}{5}$ $\frac{1}{5}$

$$+ \frac{3}{5}$$

$$\overline{\quad \frac{4}{5} \quad}$$

5.05 $14 < 18$

5.06 $68°F - 53°F = 15°F$

5.07   square

5.08   4   3

         8   6

Part One

1.01

$$\begin{array}{r} 40 \\ +\ 80 \\ \hline 123\ 120 \end{array} \qquad \begin{array}{r} 200 \\ +\ 100 \\ \hline 302\ 300 \end{array} \qquad \begin{array}{r} 4{,}000 \\ +\ 3{,}000 \\ \hline 7{,}197\ 7{,}000 \end{array} \qquad \begin{array}{r} 5{,}000 \\ +\ 3{,}000 \\ \hline 8{,}026\ 8{,}000 \end{array}$$

$$\begin{array}{r} 80 \\ -\ 30 \\ \hline 52\ 50 \end{array} \qquad \begin{array}{r} 700 \\ -\ 500 \\ \hline 196\ 200 \end{array} \qquad \begin{array}{r} 8000 \\ -\ 7000 \\ \hline 1{,}397\ 1{,}000 \end{array} \qquad \begin{array}{r} 7000 \\ -\ 4000 \\ \hline 3{,}005\ 3{,}000 \end{array}$$

1.02 4,000; 1,000; 3,000; 8,000 miles

1.03 3, 6, 9, 12, 15, 18, 21, 24, 27, 30
4, 8, 12, 16, 20, 24, 28, 32, 36, 40

1.04 $\frac{4}{5}$ $\frac{5}{7}$ $\frac{3}{3}=1$ $\frac{2}{2}=1$

1.05 $\frac{5}{9}$ $\frac{3}{12}$ $\frac{2}{10}$ $\frac{2}{8}$

Part Two

2.01 14, 1   8, 1   51, 2

2.02 4, 4, 12   3, 3, 12
3, 3, 12   2, 2, 12

2.03 617   7,174   331   3,346

2.04 20   6   24   30   45   20   80   21

Part Three

3.01

Y

N

3.02 $5\frac{3}{8}$ $8\frac{3}{3}=8+1=9$ $7\frac{3}{5}$ $2\frac{1}{6}$

3.03 10 linear feet
5 square feet

3.04 eighteen
three hundred seventy-one
six hundred five
four thousand, three

3.05 Suggested Answers:
gallon   hour

3.06 8,632   2,368

Part Four

4.01 7:50   3:07

4.02 40   300
90   500

4.03 line   end points   angle

4.04 1,000 + 500 + 10 + 10 + 10 + 5
+ 1 + 1,
M + D + X + X + X + V + I + I,
MDXXXVII

4.05

$$\begin{array}{r} 5\frac{3}{8} \\ +\ 4\frac{2}{8} \\ \hline 9\frac{5}{8} \end{array}$$

4.06 137   8,254

4.07 thousands   8,000
hundreds   700
tens   0

4.08 43   1,561

Part Five

5.01 7 + 3 + 4 = 9 + 5
14 = 14
or 7 + 3 = 9 + 5 − 4
10 = 10

5.02 16 − 8, 8
13 − 7, 6

5.03 12 square inches

5.04 1,298
east
10 cookies, 5 cookies, 7 cookies
$\frac{2}{3}$ apple
A.M. should be P.M.

5.05 XI   III   IX

LIFEPAC TEST 301

1. 0, 1, 2, 3, 4, 5, 6, 7, 8, 9

2. five hundred twenty-nine
   eight hundred four

3. 5, 18, 43, 57, 195, 356, 791, 820

4. 6, 7   5, 8, 4
   60, 7   500, 80, 4

5.

	addend		minuend
	addend		subtrahend
78	sum	21	difference

6. 15   7

7. 72   17   120   593   514   451

8. 12   36

9. feet   inches

10. $11 - 4 \neq 8$
    $0 + 6 = 6$

11. =   ≠
    <   >

12. second
    fifth

13. 7   9:28

14. 277   486   271

15. 85 pennies
    42 pennies

LIFEPAC TEST 302

1. $3 + 8 = 11$ $8 + 3 = 11$
   $11 - 3 = 8$ $11 - 8 = 3$

2. 10, 12   even

3. 17   363   815   374   37   24

4. 0   place holder

5. 7, 6, 3
   700, 60, 3

6.
```
    275            82
  + 368          - 34
   643            48
```

7. 0   5, 0
   0, 2, 4, 6, 8

8. eighteen   five hundred sixty

9.   numerator
   fraction bar
                      denominator

10.

11. five-eighths

12. >   <
    ≠   =

13. square
    flat
    circle

14. Five plus eight is not equal to fifteen.
    Fourteen minus six is less than twelve.

15. 103¢ $1.03

16. 585   789   43   61

17. 12   36   3

18. 56 cookies
    38 cookies

Math 300 Test Key

LIFEPAC TEST 303

1. $6 + 6 = 12$, $6 + 6 = 12$,
   $12 - 6 = 6$, $12 - 6 = 6$

   $0 + 5 = 5$, $5 + 0 = 5$
   $5 - 0 = 5$, $5 - 5 = 0$

2. addend   minuend
   addend   subtrahend
   sum   difference

3. 503

4. 163   836   750   47   406   583

5. 16   2,000
   16   2
   2   4

6. Suggested Answer: pound
   month

7. 249   942

8. 655   632   29   548

9. $5 < 7$
   $2 + 3 \neq 2 + 4$

10. $\frac{4}{7}$ $\frac{3}{5}$

11. $\frac{4}{12}$ $\frac{4}{6}$

12. $\frac{12}{12}$ $\frac{6}{6}$

13. midnight
    midnight
    P.M.

14. ones   3

15. $ .57 $3.65

16. 1 inch
    square

LIFEPAC TEST 304

1. thousands   tens

2. 6,394

3. 3,556   3,557   3,558   3,559   3,560

4. 13   18

5. 903   1,484   689   58   284   587

6. $\begin{array}{r} 40 \\ + 30 \\ \hline 71 \quad 70 \end{array}$

7. $1\frac{1}{4}$ $1\frac{1}{2}$

8. 3   2   12
   16   12   60

9. seven thousand, six hundred four

10. 9, 4, 6, 0
    9,000, 400, 60, 0

11. Suggested Answers:
    3   2   1   1   4
    3   6   9

12. $<$ $=$ $>$

13. $\begin{array}{r} 523 \\ 65 \\ + 8 \\ \hline 596 \end{array}$ $\begin{array}{r} 471 \\ - 246 \\ \hline 225 \end{array}$

14. 10, 10, 5, 1, 26

15. 3, 6, 9, 12, 15, 18, 21, 24, 27, 30

16.

17. $\frac{3}{9}$, $\frac{2}{9}$, $\frac{5}{9}$

18. 0
    place holder

19. two-fifths   three-eighths

20. 50 box cars
    $\frac{3}{8}$ box of chalk

LIFEPAC TEST 305

1.   8,402   8,405
    8,401   ~~8420~~ 8,403   8,404   ~~8450~~

2. 86, 102, 736, 858

3. 🥔 112   43   ⚫ 37   72

              $\underline{+\ 69}$ $\underline{-\ 35}$
              112   37

4. 1,234   1,165   377   355

5. twelfth ——————— 39
    thirty-ninth ——— 21
    eighty-first ——— 78
    seventy-eighth —— 12
    forty-fifth ——— 81
    twenty-first ——— 45

6. $\frac{4}{5}$ $\frac{11}{12}$ $\frac{3}{8}$ $\frac{5}{9}$

7. 32   212

8. $2\frac{3}{4}$

9. **How Much Do Pet Dogs Weigh?**

    Patsy's dog
    Loren's dog
    0 10 20 30 40 50 60 70 80 90 100
    pounds

10. Eight plus three is greater than five
       plus two.
    Nine minus seven is not equal to six
       minus three.

11.   500
        $\underline{+\ 400}$
      909   900

12. 3, 1, 3, 1, 8

13. Lines of symmetry may vary.

    hexagon   pentagon   octagon

14. even, odd

15. X + X − I, 10 + 10 − 1, 19

16. 16

17. Suggested Answer:
        2 dollars, 1 quarter, 3 pennies

18. August 8

LIFEPAC TEST 306

1. 7,584 7,533 6,853 387 557 1,223

2. 2, 4, 6, 8, 10, 12, 14, 16, 18, 20

3. 76   87
    O, O, E, yes   E, O, O, yes

4. 60   24
    36   365
    144   9

5. 16 linear feet
    15 square feet

6. 256   6,520

7. $\frac{3}{7}$ $\frac{7}{9}$
     $\underline{+\ \frac{2}{7}}$ $\underline{-\ \frac{4}{9}}$
        $\frac{5}{7}$ $\frac{3}{9}$

8. ≠   ≠   >   <

9. $\frac{1}{2}$ $\frac{2}{4}$

10. $1.65
    $\underline{+\ \$\ .48}$
      $2.13

11. L + X + X + X − I,
      50 + 10 + 10 + 10 − 1, 79

12.   80   200
       $\underline{+\ 40}$ $\underline{+\ 500}$
    115 120   726 700

13. 5 + 3 = 16 − 8
    30 < 46

14. **Counting Cars**

    10
    8
    6
    4
    2
    0
       blue   green   white

15.

16. 130

17. eight thousand, fifty-four

18. $2.02

LIFEPAC TEST 307

1. 8   16   15   25

2. five-sevenths
   two and four-ninths

3. 7,569   9,302   4,825   834

4. 508   266   3,921   2,747

5. 12   5,280
   144   9

6. 12 linear inches, 5 square inches

7. $7\frac{5}{6}$ $3\frac{4}{8}$

8. 32   33
   O, O, E, yes   E, O, O, yes

9. $50 - 1$, L − I, IL
   $50 + 10 + 10 + 5 + 1$,
      L + X + X + V + I, LXXVI

10.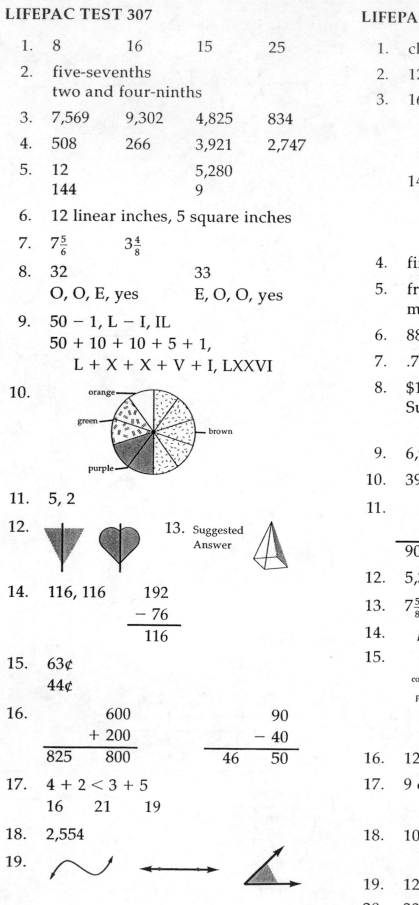

11. 5, 2

12.

13. Suggested Answer

14. 116, 116   192
              − 76
              116

15. 63¢
   44¢

16.   600   90
   + 200   − 40
   825 800   46   50

17. $4 + 2 < 3 + 5$
   16   21   19

18. 2,554

19.

LIFEPAC TEST 308

1. closed lines, faces, Angles

2. 12   8

3. 16   13   75   13
          + 46 − 59   46
           59   16 + 16
                       75

    141   427   953   427
         + 385 − 812 385
          812   141 + 141
                       953

4. fifth

5. fraction, seven-eighths
   mixed number, three and one-fourth

6. 88   odd, odd, even

7. .7   seven-tenths

8. $1.57
   Suggested Answer:
      1 dollar, 2 quarters, 1 nickel, 2 pennies

9. 6,935   5,673   1,342   1,630

10. 392   6,002   2,328   2,118

11.   700   700
   + 200   − 300
   906 900   427 400

12. 5,306   8,001

13. $7\frac{5}{8}$ $5\frac{2}{2} = 5+1 = 6$ $8\frac{3}{3} = 8 + 1 = 9$ $5\frac{5}{7}$

14. ↑ ↓ → ←

15.
   oatmeal
   cornflakes
   pancakes
   toast
   0 1 2 3 4 5 6 7 8

16. 12 15 12 70

17. 9 cones

18. $100 + 100 + 50 + 10 + 5 - 1$
      C + C + L + X + V − I, CCLXIV

19. 12 linear feet, 5 square feet

20. 23   27   22

LIFEPAC TEST 309

1. 9 8 12 15 11 7 8 9 6 9

2. ⬚ or ⬚

3. angle
   line segment
   perimeter
   curved line

4. seven-eighths $\frac{5}{9}$
   nine and one-third $4\frac{2}{7}$

5.

   Y

   Y

6.
96	4,053	541	4,302
248	618	− 63	−1,568
+ 7	+ 51	478	2,734
351	4,722		

7. <   =   <

8. 32   0

9. square   pyramid   cube   diamond

10. $\frac{8}{8}=1$ $\frac{2}{5}$ $7\frac{3}{3}=7+1=8$ $4\frac{4}{7}$

11. 14   24   9   40
    6   20   50 14
         90   40

12. 7 square feet

13. four thousand, seven hundred nine

14. 6,000   8,000   10,000

15. 500 + 50 − 10 + 5 + 1 + 1 + 1,
    D + L − X + V + I + I + I, DXLVIII

16. 48   32

17. 15, 20, 40, 35, 10

LIFEPAC TEST 310

1.
300	5,000	400	7,000
+500	+3,000	−200	−3,000
821 800	8,267 8,000	225 200	4,446 4,000

2. 1,000; 2,000; 3,000; 6,000 books

3. 3, 6, 9, 12, 15, 18, 21, 24, 27, 30
   4, 8, 12, 16, 20, 24, 28, 32, 36, 40

4. $\frac{4}{8}$ $\frac{7}{7}=1$ $\frac{2}{9}$ $\frac{6}{12}$
   $4\frac{4}{5}$ $7\frac{3}{3}=7+1=8$ $4\frac{1}{8}$ $3\frac{2}{6}$

5. 87, 2   62, 1

6. 2, 2, 12   5, 5, 12
   4, 4, 12   1, 1, 12

7. 1,127   8,475   348   2,445

8. 25   21   40   6   24   45   80   12

9. 12 linear yards, 6 square yards

10. three hundred seventy-one
    nine thousand, eight hundred three

11. Suggested Answers:
    gallon   mile

12. line segment
    angle
    width
    end points

13. 1,000 + 1,000 + 100 + 50 + 10 + 5 − 1,
    M + M + C + L + X + V − I,
    MMCLXIV

14. 4 + 9 + 2 = 7 + 8
            15 = 15
    or 4 + 9 = 7 + 8 − 2
            13 = 13

15. 14 − 10, 4

16. a. 931
    b. 4:30 P.M.   4:40 P.M.   4:15 P.M.
    c. $\frac{1}{4}$ candy bar

ALTERNATE LIFEPAC TEST 301

1. 0, 1, 2, 3, 4, 5, 6, 7, 8, 9

2. seven hundred three
   nine hundred sixty-one

3. 3, 17, 38, 72, 204, 430, 600, 931

4. 8, 6   2, 7, 6
   80, 6   200, 70, 6

5.

	addend		minuend
	addend		subtrahend
96	sum	23	difference

6. 6   19

7. 42   16   103   682   427   733

8. 12   36

9. feet   inches

10. $5 + 4 = 9$
    $7 - 3 \neq 5$

11. $=$ $\neq$
    $>$ $<$

12. third
    fifth

13. 7   4:58

14. 498   685   441

15. 58 rocks
    40 rocks

ALTERNATE LIFEPAC TEST 302

1. $6 + 7 = 13$ $7 + 6 = 13$
   $13 - 6 = 7$ $13 - 7 = 6$

2. 11, 13   odd

3. 17   627   932   525   16   15

4. 500   place holder

5. 8, 0, 4
   800, 0, 4

6.

75	632
$- 57$	$+ 151$
18	783

7. 0   0, 5
   0, 2, 4, 6, 8

8. thirteen   three hundred eighty

9.   numerator
   fraction bar
            denominator

10.

11. three-sevenths

12. $<$ $<$
    $\neq$ $=$

13. triangle
    flat
    circle

14. Three plus six is not equal to twelve.
    Eighteen minus nine is greater than
    seven.

15. 112¢ $1.12

16. 657   779   45   21

17. 12   36   3

18. 36
    20

Math 300 Alternate Test Key

ALTERNATE LIFEPAC TEST 303

1. $7 + 0 = 7, 0 + 7 = 7,$
   $7 - 0 = 7, 7 - 7 = 0$
   $8 + 8 = 16, 8 + 8 = 16$
   $16 - 8 = 8, 16 - 8 = 8$

2. addend   minuend
   addend   subtrahend
   sum   difference

3. 806

4. 146   651   720   47   257   355

5. 16   2,000
   16   2
   2   4

6. ounces/cup
   pounds

7. 631   136

8. 804   645   47   515

9. $4 + 2 \neq 4 + 3$
   6 people > 4 people

10. $\frac{2}{8}$ $\frac{5}{9}$

11. $\frac{3}{10}$ $\frac{2}{7}$

12. $\frac{10}{10}$ $\frac{7}{7}$

13. midnight
    midnight
    A.M.

14. tens   30

15. 50¢ $1.28

16. 2 inches
    rectangle

ALTERNATE LIFEPAC TEST 304

1. hundreds   thousands

2. 5,674

3. 6,237   6,238   6,239   6,240   6,241

4. 17   19

5. 830   1,086   789   24   265   283

6. $\begin{array}{r} 40 \\ +\,30 \\ \hline 71 \quad 70 \end{array}$

7. $1\frac{1}{2}$ $2\frac{3}{4}$

8. 3   2   12
   16   12   60

9. six thousand, three hundred two

10. 2, 5, 6, 3
    2,000, 500, 60, 3

11. Suggested Answers:
    4   1   1   2
    4   3   1   2

12. >   =   <

13. $\begin{array}{r} 426 \\ 58 \\ +\,7 \\ \hline 491 \end{array}$ $\begin{array}{r} 632 \\ -\,147 \\ \hline 485 \end{array}$

14. 10, 5, 1, 1, 17

15. 3, 6, 9, 12, 15, 18, 21, 24, 27, 30

16.

17. $\frac{3}{6}, \frac{1}{6}, \frac{4}{6}$

18. 0
    place holder

19. one-third   two-sixths

20. 50 leaves
    $\frac{4}{12}$

ALTERNATE LIFEPAC TEST 305

1.   6,323   6,325
   6,321   6,322   ~~6,332~~   6,324   ~~6,352~~

2. 36, 108, 424, 252

3.   102   65   45   91
             + 37   − 46
              102   45

4. 1,124   1,120   668   157

5. forty-sixth   92
   twenty-ninth   46
   sixty-third   15
   ninety-second   63
   seventy-eighth   29
   fifteenth   78

6. $\frac{6}{9}$ $\frac{5}{8}$ $\frac{4}{6}$ $\frac{3}{9}$

7. 32   212

8. $3\frac{1}{4}$

9.

10. Six plus eight is less than nine plus nine.
    Eight minus zero is equal to four plus four.

11.   400
          + 200
       603   600

12. 2, 1, 2, 1, 6

13. Lines of symmetry may vary.

   pentagon   hexagon   octagon

14. odd, even

15. X + X + V − I, 10 + 10 + 5 − 1, 24

16. 5

17. Suggested Answer:
    3 dollars, 2 dimes, 1 nickel, 4 pennies

18. August 9

ALTERNATE LIFEPAC TEST 306

1. 5,381   3,915   6,551   437   408   5,221

2. 2, 4, 6, 8, 10, 12, 14, 16, 18, 20

3. 57   96
   O, E, O, yes   E, E, E, yes

4. 60   24
   36   365
   144   9

5. 12 linear feet, 9 square feet

6. 7,530   357

7. $\frac{2}{5}$ $\frac{9}{12}$
     $+ \frac{1}{5}$ $- \frac{5}{12}$
         $\frac{3}{5}$ $\frac{4}{12}$

8. ≠   ≠   >   <

9. $\frac{1}{2}$ $\frac{3}{6}$

10. $1.23
    + $ .42
       $1.65

11. L + X + V − I,
    50 + 10 + 5 − 1, 64

12.   70   400
       + 80   + 600
    148   150   999   1,000

13. 16 − 8 = 8 + 0
    85 > 58

14.

15.

16. 110

17. three thousand, sixty-one

18. 35¢

Math 300 Alternate Test Key

ALTERNATE LIFEPAC TEST 307

1. 12   6   20   40

2. four-eighths
   three and one-third

3. 6,439   7,035   8,612   847

4. 467   157   4,845   4,728

5. 12   5,280
   144   9

6. 12 linear inches, 5 square inches

7. $8\frac{6}{7}$ $2\frac{3}{9}$

8. 28   33
   E, E, E, yes   E, O, O, yes

9. 10 + 10 + 10 + 5 + 1,
      X + X + X + V + I, XXXVI
   50 + 10 + 10 + 10 + 5 − 1,
      L + X + X + X + V − I, LXXXIV

10.

11. 3, 2

12.   13. Suggested Answer

14. 69, 69   152
                    − 83
                    69

15. 67¢
    23¢

16. 800   80
       + 200   − 30
    1,027   1,000   46   50

17. 6 + 8 < 9 + 6
    12   9   7

18. 3,000

19.

ALTERNATE LIFEPAC TEST 308

1. closed lines, angles, faces

2. 9   4

3. 16   18   63   18
         + 29   − 47   29
          47   16   + 16
                        63

   260   136   681   136
         + 285   − 421   285
          421   260   + 260
                        681

4. seventh

5. fraction, six-eighths
   mixed number, four and two-fifths

6. 77   even, odd, odd

7. .3   three-tenths

8. $1.38
   Suggested Answer:
      1 dollar, 1 quarter, 1 dime, 3 pennies

9. 8,052   6,319   1,223   1,249

10. 409   4,002   1,362   1,477

11. 500   800
       + 400   − 400
    909   900   402   400

12. 2,051   7,004

13. $8\frac{3}{3} = 8+1 = 9$ $9\frac{4}{8}$ $6\frac{2}{2} = 6+1 = 7$ $9\frac{7}{9}$

14. ←   ↓   →   ↑

15.

16. 16   35   9   40

17. 8 cones

18. 100 + 100 + 10 + 10 + 5 − 1
       C + C + X + X + V − I,   CCXXIV

19. 10 linear yards, 5 square yards

20. 23   24   26

ALTERNATE LIFEPAC TEST 309

1. 11 11 9 7 16 6 9 3 2 7

2.

3. line segment
   curved line
   perimeter
   angle

4. six-sevenths $\frac{3}{8}$
   two and three-fifths $5\frac{4}{6}$

5.
   Y
   Y

6.
47	2,873	632	5,120
361	705	− 85	− 2,365
+ 9	+ 39	547	2,755
417	3,617		

7. < ≠ >

8. 212 100

9. cylinder rectangle pyramid oval

10. $\frac{5}{7}$ $\frac{6}{10}$ $8\frac{5}{5} = 8 + 1 = 9$ $3\frac{4}{8}$

11. 16 28 6 35
    27 30 30 12
        70 20

12. 6 square yards

13. three thousand, fifty-two

14. 5,000 8,000 2,000

15. 500 + 100 + 10 + 5 − 1,
    D + C + X + V − I, DCXIV

16. 21 4,000

17. 25, 30, 15, 40, 30

ALTERNATE LIFEPAC TEST 310

1.
300	7,000	900	7,000
+200	+1,000	−600	−2,000
527 500	8,133 8,000	340 300	4,766 5,000

2. 2,000; 2,000; 5,000; 9,000 books

3. 3, 6, 9, 12, 15, 18, 21, 24, 27, 30
   4, 8, 12, 16, 20, 24, 28, 32, 36, 40

4. $\frac{6}{9}$ $\frac{5}{5} = 1$ $\frac{6}{10}$ $\frac{2}{16}$
   $6\frac{2}{2} = 6 + 1 = 7$ $9\frac{7}{8}$ $2\frac{4}{12}$ $1\frac{1}{3}$

5. 58, 1 15, 2

6. 4, 4, 12 3, 3, 12
   2, 2, 12 3, 3, 12

7. 1,123 8,310 314 3,758

8. 15 28 50 30 30 27 16 16

9. 10 linear feet, 4 square feet

10. four hundred fifty-six
    three thousand, fifty-four

11. Suggested Answers:
    minutes miles

12. end points
    line segment
    width
    angle

13. 1,000 + 100 + 100 + 50 + 10 − 1,
    M + C + C + L + X − I,
    MCCLIX

14. 3 + 6 + 2 = 4 + 7
    11 = 11
    or 3 + 6 = 4 + 7 − 2
    9 = 9

15. 18 + 5, 23

16. 106
    April 8 April 3 April 12
    $\frac{3}{8}$ of the book